Facilitating and Training in

Quality Function Deployment

© 1991 **GOAL/QPC**
Published by GOAL/QPC
13 Branch Street
Methuen, Massachusetts 01844
10 9 8 7 6 5 4
First Edition

ISBN 1-879364-18-2

Table of Contents

Facilitating and Training in Quality Function Deployment

		Page
Preface		vii
1	Facilitating Quality Function Deployment	1
2	Tips for Facilitating Successful Quality Function Deployment Meetings	3
3	Introducing Quality Function Deployment to Your Organization	7
4	History of Quality Function Deployment	17
5	Overview of Quality Function Deployment	21
6	Lessons to be Learned	43
7	The Wallace Wallet Works Case Study	49
8	Understanding the Voice of the Customer	59
9	Matrix of Matrices Flow: The Tool Box	67
10	Wallace Wallet Works Case Study	73
11	Reviewing Chart A-1	111
12	Using Software	121
13	Supplementary QFD Case Study	133
14	Summary	143
Glossary		145
Index		149

The authors would like to thank the following individuals for their guidance, contribution, support, and many critiques in the development of this text:

Robert C. Porter
Vice President,
Materials and Controls Group,
Quality and Reliability Assurance,
Texas Instruments

for helping us keep our focus on the importance of maintaining clarity for the roles of management, facilitators, and program managers in the QFD process.

George Murray,
Director, Quality Technologies Institute,
Polaroid Corporation

for his help in maintaining the continuity between chapters.

Lawrence L. Domonkos,
Manager,
Training Requirements and Delivery,
United States Marketing Group,
Xerox Corporation

for helping us focus on the design of effective QFD training.

Mike DeNoma,
Division Marketing Director,
Citibank N.A.,
Singapore

for his help in validating this approach to banking and service organizations.

Michele Kierstead,
Director of Publications and Graphics,
GOAL/QPC

Steven Boudreau,
Publishing Consultant/Systems Administrator,
GOAL/QPC

Karen Jamrog,
Writer/Editor,
GOAL/QPC

Cheryl DeCristofaro,
Graphic Designer,
GOAL/QPC

for their patience, dedication, and creative input.

Preface

This book is focused on the facilitation and training of Quality Function Deployment (QFD). It is written with the premise that the reader is knowledgeable of QFD methodology.

The information in this book prepares the facilitator or trainer to educate an organization in the benefits and power of QFD. This education and training can take place either before the QFD project begins, in a structured classroom environment, or using a just-in-time approach as the team proceeds with the project. This training can be accomplished by the facilitator, an in-house expert, or an outside consultant. This text will provide the facilitator or trainer with guidance in the following:

1. Introducing the concepts of QFD.

2. Developing the strategy for implementing QFD.

3. Organizing QFD teams.

4. Training QFD teams.

5. Facilitating QFD projects.

Individuals who will facilitate QFD teams must have certain commitments from their management. These commitments are a contract in terms of the role management must play. The role of management in the QFD process, while equally clear, is less understood than that of the facilitator and has not been documented.

Management's role in the QFD process is to:

1. Understand the QFD process.

2. Define the purpose of the QFD project.

3. Prioritize and plan which projects the QFD process will be used on:
   - Who
   - What
   - When
   - Why
   - Where
   - How

4. Develop for the selected QFD projects:
   - Objectives
   - Scope
   - Expectations
   - Goals

5. Appoint a program manager for the project selected for QFD analysis. This program manager is responsible for driving the QFD study and integrating it into the product development process. This responsibility should not be delegated to the facilitator.

   The program manager responsible for the team's success needs a facilitator to assist. The facilitator's function is to make certain the QFD effort goes smoothly, coordinate and set up the meetings, help the program manager surmount hurdles, prevent wheel-spinning, and keep the project on track.

6. Top management and the program manager must pick the members of the QFD study team, including the facilitator.

7. Management must provide the QFD team with a charter for the project. This should be a written statement describing:
   - Goals
   - Objectives
   - Expectations
   - Scope

8. Management must empower the QFD team, which includes giving:
   - Power
   - Permission
   - Protection

9. Management must be committed and involved in the QFD process. This includes asking relevant questions, such as:
   - How did you determine who the customer is?
   - How did you determine demanded quality?
   - How did you do competitive analysis?
   - When did you last survey your customer?
   - What are the major conclusions from the study?

When management selects individuals to become facilitators, it should develop a profile of characteristics including:
   - People skills
   - Experience
   - Expertise
   - Organizational ability
   - Negotiating skills

This text was written for those selected by their management to facilitate and train in the QFD process. It is a compilation of the authors' experiences of facilitating and training many organizations in Quality Function Deployment.

Chapter 1

Facilitating Quality Function Deployment

Introduction

Quality Function Deployment (QFD) is a Cross-Functional Management team approach to developing new products or services or for upgrading existing ones.

Proper facilitation of the team effort is critical for successful completion of a QFD study that results in breakthroughs and insights for the QFD team. Proper facilitation will help a QFD team fully integrate the talents, skills, and creative potential of each team member. One of the key tasks a facilitator has to accomplish with the QFD teams and the organization as a whole is to explain what QFD is and its organizational benefits.

The QFD facilitator has a coordinator's role in the planning, design, execution, and completion of the QFD project. Unfortunately, this role is often not visible, and as such, has not been properly valued by organizations using QFD. The value of group facilitators will emerge in the near future as more organizations adopt Total Quality Management (TQM) as their new management structure. In the future those training in and writing about QFD should provide their audience with an in-depth treatment of the QFD project team facilitator's role and value.

Quality Function Deployment

Quality Function Deployment is a structured and disciplined process that provides a means to identify and carry the voice of the customer through each stage of product development and implementation. This process can be deployed horizontally through marketing, product planning, engineering, manufacturing, service, and all other departments in your organization involved in product development.

QFD enables organizations to prioritize customer demands, develop innovative responses to those needs, and orchestrate a successful implementation involving all departments. QFD is a planning tool that carries the voice of the customer all the way through product development, to manufacturing, and into the marketplace. QFD focuses on planning and problem prevention early in the product development process, thereby reducing design errors, which results in fewer problems in production.

QFD's claim of "better designs in half the time" is attracting strong interest from dozens of large- and intermediate-sized companies. It makes the design and marketing of new products easier. Some examples of QFD applications include:

- 28% reduction in new product development cycle time
  — Texas Instruments, Materials and Controls Group, Attleboro, MA

- Clarification of engineering requirements
  — Ford Light Truck

- Improved sales
  — Procter & Gamble hotel products

- Improved internal customer/supplier relationship
  — Digital Equipment Corporation

- Improved external customer/supplier relationship
  — Ford Climate Control, Cirtek, General Electric

- Improved manufacturing documentation and control
  — General Electric

- Improved hardware and software design
  — Hewlett-Packard and Digital Equipment Corporation

- Improved new product design and launch
  — Masland and Deere & Company

- Clarification and prioritization of customer demands
  — Digital Equipment Corporation

- Customer-driven quality characteristics and quality in daily work
  — Florida Power & Light

- Understanding who the customers are
  — Polaroid

- Multi-company new product development
  — Rockwell International

Some of the benefits of QFD are:
- Fewer engineering changes
- Faster time cycle to market
- Decreased cost
- Improved quality
- Satisfied customers
- Clearly understood customer(s)
- Improved documentation
- Focused customer requirements
- Effectively used competitive information
- Identified key action elements
- Identified gaps and missing elements
- Prioritized available resources

There are also some intangible benefits that are difficult to quantify, yet are perceived by the QFD team and the organization. Among the intangible benefits are:

- Improved cross-functional communication
- Team building
- Development of a common language base
- Dynamic documentation that can be updated as new information is available
- Expanded global, rather than myopic thinking

Chapter 2

Tips for Facilitating Successful QFD Meetings

The QFD team facilitator is an important ingredient in a successful QFD team. This facilitation role is frequently overlooked or hidden when the team is successful, but often comes to the forefront if the team is unsuccessful.

The QFD team facilitator has six vital roles to perform in a QFD study:

Planner
- Help the team establish objectives
- Develop agenda
- Establish dates, times, and places for meetings
- Facilitate meeting room setup; logistics

Guide
- Explain the process
- Regulate the flow of the process
- Keep the group focused on the QFD process
- Monitor participation; keep everyone involved

Cheerleader
- Provide motivation
- Introduce QFD
- Make group work visible on flip charts, on QFD charts, and other means available

Coach
- Develop the team
- Train the team in the QFD process
- Help the team decide which matrices to use
- Help the team to continuously improve its process
- Facilitate consensus decision making

Arbitrator
- Help settle disputes and conflicts — collaborative effort
- Keep the team spirit alive
- Ensure problems are being solved
- Avoid being manipulative
- Refrain from forcing your ideas on the team or fighting for them
- Build trust

Soothsayer
- Try to foresee future problems
- Look for patterns in the participants' behavior that may interfere with group performance

The function of the QFD team facilitator is to be a neutral, non-evaluative, and non-manipulative group focal point. A key attribute of a good facilitator is to keep the group on track to its objectives and prevent it from getting bogged down or distracted.

The QFD team facilitator should allow time at the end of each session to provide constructive feedback. This provides a focus for the team on behavior that is beneficial to the task. This is an important part of the coaching role and will help the team clearly understand the problem it is focusing on. At the end of each session the facilitator should summarize the results of the meeting, the tasks to be accomplished for the next meeting, who is responsible for each task, and what the group will be doing in the next session.

A QFD team facilitator should clearly understand the QFD process in detail and know the Seven Basic Quality Control Tools and Seven Management and Planning Tools. In addition to these technical tools, the facilitator should also be skilled in some basic organizational development tools such as listening, communication, and team building.

Facilitator Checklist for an Effective Meeting

Pre-Meeting
- Plan Who, What, When, Where, Why, and How Many attendees.
- Determine the appropriate composition of the team.
- Secure a facility that can accommodate the attendees comfortably, has breakout rooms, and plenty of wall space to display the QFD charts as they develop.
- Obtain all the necessary equipment and supplies to conduct the training session or the QFD project.
- Publish a detailed agenda in advance of the meeting and distribute to all attendees and their organizational supervisors.

- Ensure that the facility is set up properly before the meeting begins.
- Verify attendees' intentions.

Meeting Start
- Start on time and end on time.
- Have participants introduce each other.
- Review the agenda.
- Revise if necessary.
- Stick to the agenda.
- Manage time effectively; set time limits.
- Review action items from the previous meeting.
- Solicit full participation.
- Record decisions; capture the group memory.
  Note: The facilitator's role is to keep the meeting focused and moving while remaining neutral.

During the Meeting
Encourage participants to:
- Feedback their perception of what was said.
- Be non-judgmental — just listen carefully.
- Ask direct, not loaded questions.
- Talk openly.
- Ask neutral questions, e.g., "Can you give me some examples?"
- Ask questions to help the speaker clarify his/her thoughts.
- Listen for both the "facts" and the "feeling" in the person's statement.
- Give feedback in their own words.
- Try to understand the message, not judge the person.

Meeting End
- Identify tasks to be accomplished for the next meeting.

- Determine who is responsible for completing the tasks.
- Establish the next meeting time, place, agenda, and participants.
- Evaluate the meeting using a plus and minus T-chart.

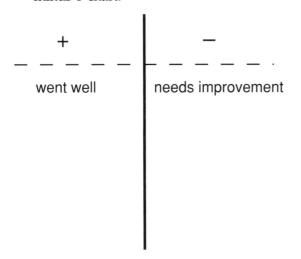

Agree as a group on how to plan and improve for the next meeting by removing the negatives. Remember meetings are processes that should be subjected to continuous improvement.

The facilitator should issue a summary memo soon after the meeting and well in advance of the next meeting.

Chapter 3

Introducing Quality Function Deployment to Your Organization

Introducing Quality Function Deployment into an ongoing product and service design and redesign process is usually a difficult task. The current product and service development process usually has been in place for quite a while and any change, even if only suggested, will not be received with cordial welcome.

Your current system of product and service design and development has its own culture. The people in the design and development system have acquired comfortable, predictable habits. Turf battles have been settled in the distant past and the system may be in a state of equilibrium. Everyone in the system accommodates and compromises constantly to hold this equilibrium state. The equilibrium state equates to the "Don't Rock the Boat Syndrome" and prevents those in the

system from investigating new ideas because new ideas are perceived as threats to the status quo.

The QFD team facilitator needs to assist the design and development division in an assessment of its current strengths and weaknesses before attempting to introduce the Quality Function Deployment technology. This assessment process is a self-study in the division to establish a baseline, to describe visually the design and development's position on the many facets of its mission. Through the baselining process, the leaders of the design and development organization develop a consensual picture. To accomplish this baselining process in a design and development division, the following Quality Function Deployment Readiness Assessment has been developed.

Quality Function Deployment Readiness Assessment

SD	Strongly Disagree
D	Disagree
A	Agree
SA	Strongly Agree

SD	D	A	SA

1. As an organization we clearly know who our customers are, internally and externally.

    —|———|———|———|—

2. We fully understand our customer's wants, needs, and expectations.

    —|———|———|———|—

3. We consistently meet and/or exceed our customer's needs in our designs.

    —|———|———|———|—

4. Marketing delivers a complete product definition with the market requirements clearly defined based upon customer needs.

    —|———|———|———|—

5. Changes are a rare occurrence after a new product is introduced.

    —|———|———|———|—

6. We understand our current processes' capabilities and constraints.

    —|———|———|———|—

Quality Function Deployment Readiness Assessment

Quality Function Deployment Readiness Assessment

SD Strongly Disagree
D   Disagree
A   Agree
SA Strongly Agree

SD	D	A	SA

7. Our design and development process is totally integrated, from Planning to Design to Production to Sales and Service.

8. We design products that are geared toward ease of production.

9. We have few design-related delays during new product introduction.

10. We have a communication process that translates customer wants through the entire organization without distortion.

11. Our designs minimize the probability of returned units and high warranty costs.

Quality Function Deployment Readiness Assessment

SD   Strongly Disagree
D   Disagree
A   Agree
SA   Strongly Agree

SD	D	A	SA

12. Our design and development process is totally focused on customer satisfaction; it is not internally focused.

13. All employees are focused on obtaining an understanding of customer needs and wants and then meeting or exceeding them.

A radar chart, shown in figure 3-1, is a technique that can be used to record the group's assessment of each question. Each spoke on the radar chart represents one of the 13 questions in the QFD Readiness Assessment. The scale of measurement is such that the farther from the center of the chart, the better the score.

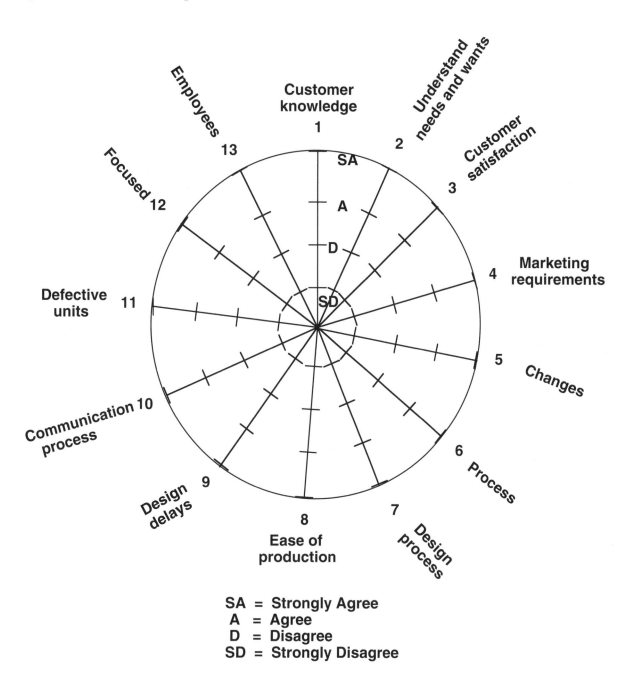

SA = Strongly Agree
A = Agree
D = Disagree
SD = Strongly Disagree

Figure 3-1. Radar Chart

The facilitator of the Quality Function Deployment Readiness Assessment should plan a four-hour session with the leaders of the design and development organization to complete this instrument. During this assessment session the facilitator should encourage the leaders to develop a holistic, organizational view rather than a myopic one centered on their specialty or expertise. The facilitator must elicit and encourage opinions and views from everyone present.

The facilitator should mark on the radar chart the consensus score for each question. During this assessment process occasionally "pockets of excellence" are identified. A pocket of excellence identifies where one or more organizational units within the system have an outstanding record on a particular criterion while the organization as a whole is doing poorly. The facilitator should capture these pockets of excellence on the radar chart with a contrasting color and make a note at the bottom of the chart for more detail.

It is a common practice for individuals in the assessment group to feel that they must defend their organizational unit against another unit's pocket of excellence. This is an unproductive task and will detract from the process' open and frank nature. Facilitators need to discourage the group members from defending their turf, and should point out that pockets of excellence are areas where the entire group can learn and should be shared with the organization as a whole to help with the improvement process.

After each of the Readiness Assessment questions are scored, the facilitator can now connect the individual dots representing the group's consensus. Pockets of excellence are not connected in the graph, but left as individual points. Usually only one or two pockets of excellence are identified. The connection of the dots results in a visual picture of the organization now, clearly showing its strengths and weaknesses as shown in figure 3-2.

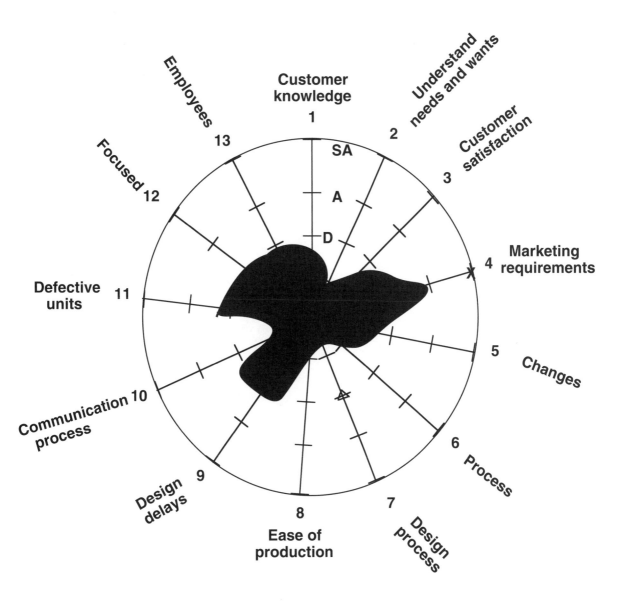

Legend:

SA = Strongly Agree
A = Agree
D = Disagree
SD = Strongly Disagree

• Pocket of Excellence

X Local Sales Office
△ CAD Group

Figure 3-2. Radar Graph with Readiness Assessment

The next step in the process is to do a sanity check with others in the organization as well as customers. Members of the assessment group can do this same exercise with members of their staff to get an assessment picture of how their organizational units envision the strengths and weaknesses of the system. Once the picture of the organization has been fine-tuned, the next step is to develop a plan for improvement. This improvement plan can also be denoted on the radar chart as shown in figure 3-3.

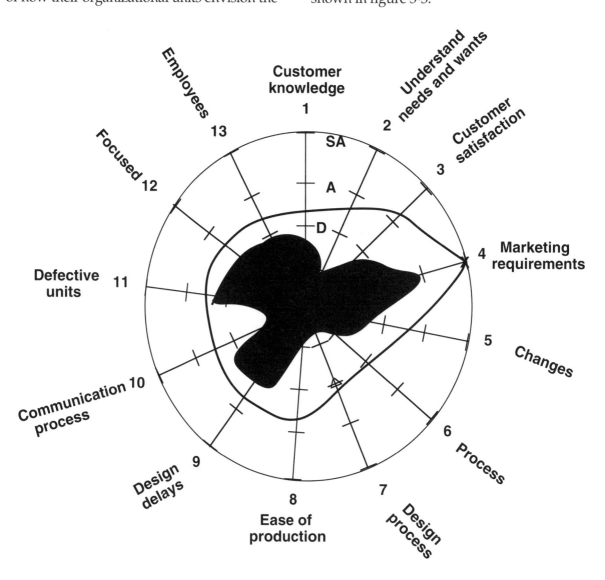

SA = Strongly Agree
A = Agree
D = Disagree
SD = Strongly Disagree

• Pocket of Excellence

X Local Sales Office
△ CAD Group

Figure 3-3. Radar Chart with Improvement Plan

This plan for the future can be in terms of the near future (12 to 18 months) or the distant future (three to five years). The improvement planning process needs to involve many members of the organization at various levels. The leaders of the organization could institute a Quality Improvement Team (QIT) around each of the assessment criteria and have the QIT develop a plan of how the improvements could be accomplished in the desired time frame. These teams need to be trained in the Quality Improvement Process before they begin their tasks. Since it is beyond the scope of this book to develop the QIT process, the following excellent references on teaming tools and techniques are provided.

The visual image developed through baselining is not static. The image will change as the organization transforms itself, as consumer demands change, and as employees become empowered. It is important to continually monitor the change on a periodic basis by developing new measurement criteria that represent the demands that will be placed on the organization in the future.

The baselining process prepares the leadership of the design and development division to receive the concepts of Quality Function Deployment in an open, objective, and receptive manner. QFD will now be initially viewed not as a threat but rather as a process that helps improve the current process' weaknesses, and adds to its strengths.

Quality Improvement Teaming, Techniques, and Tools references:

A Guide to Graphical Problem Solving, J. Moran, R. Talbot, and R. Benson. Quality Press, Milwaukee, WI, 1990.

Daily Management, J. Moran, C. Collett, and C. Cote. GOAL/QPC, Methuen, MA, 1991.

The Memory Jogger™, GOAL/QPC, Methuen, MA, 1988.

The Memory Jogger Plus+™, M. Brassard. GOAL/QPC, Methuen, MA, 1989.

The Team Handbook, P. Scholtes. Joiner Associates, Inc., Madison, WI, 1988.

After this baselining process is completed, the facilitator should introduce the concepts of QFD to the evaluation group. The following one-day overview is suggested:

Quality Function Deployment (QFD)
One-Day Overview

A.M.   History of QFD
       QFD and TQM
       Why QFD?
       Definition of QFD
       QFD Features
       Organizing for QFD
       Comprehensive QFD Model
       QFD Matrix of Matrices
       Voice of the Customer
       Tools of QFD
       • Voice of the Customer Table
       • Tree Diagrams
       • Matrix Diagram
       Customer Satisfaction Concepts
       Introduction to Chart A-1 (House of Quality)
       Case Study Introduction (Wallace Wallet Works)

       Lunch

P.M.   Constructing Chart A-1 on the Case Study
       Other QFD Charts (What are the next steps?)
       Lessons Learned in Applying QFD

The next chapter will provide the content of this course.

Chapter 4

History of Quality Function Deployment

A key component or module of any introductory briefing or comprehensive training program on Quality Function Deployment is a review of its history. This historical perspective should cover the incubation, development, and growth periods of Quality Function Deployment. The historical summary presented in this chapter details the critical dates and occurrences that contributed to the development of the process now known as Quality Function Deployment.

The facilitator or trainer will find that members of his or her audience appreciate a historical perspective of the topic being presented since it answers the following questions for them:
- HOW did it develop?
- WHY was it developed?
- WHEN did it start?
- WHERE did it start?
- WHO were the key developers?

In addition, most audience members are interested in answers to the following questions about organizations currently using

Quality Function Deployment:
- WHO is using this process?
- WHY are they using this process?
- WHEN did they start using this process?
- WHAT are the benefits they are experiencing from using this process?
- WHAT are the results they are achieving from this process?
- WHERE are they using this process in their organization?
- HOW is this process maturing?

Chapters 1, 5, and 6 contain reference material that a facilitator or trainer can use as an overview that will answer the above questions about organizations currently using Quality Function Deployment.

The historical and current perspective of Quality Function Deployment builds a basis of credibility for the process and provides a foundation for the remainder of the training. This review of the historical and current developments helps validate Quality Function Deployment for most non-believers.

History of Quality Function Deployment

1966 Japanese industry begins to formalize and use approaches to Quality Deployment based upon concepts introduced by Yoji Akao.

Bridgestone's Kurume factory introduces the listing of processing assurance items ("quality characteristics").

1969 Katsuyoshi Ishihara introduces the concept of "Function Deployment of Business" at Matsushita.

1972 Yoji Akao presents detailed methods of Quality Deployment. Introduction of "Quality Tables" at the Kobe shipyards.

1975 The computer research committee of the Japan Society for Quality Control studies Deployment of the Quality Function.

1978 The Japan Society for Quality Control forms a separate research committee to study Quality Function Deployment.

Dr. Shigeru Mizuno and Dr. Yoji Akao publish "Deployment of the Quality Function."

1980 Kayaba wins the Deming Prize with special recognition for its QFD using Furukawa's approach for bottleneck engineering.

1983 Cambridge Corporation of Tokyo, under the leadership of Masaaki Imai, introduces QFD in Chicago featuring Akao, Furukawa, and Kogure from Japan.

1984 Dr. Donald Clausing of Xerox introduces the operating mechanisms of QFD to Ford.

GOAL/QPC offers a one-day course on QFD.

1985 Lawrence Sullivan and John McHugh set up a QFD project involving Ford Body and Assembly and its suppliers.

1986 GOAL/QPC introduces Akao's materials in its five-day QFD course.

American Supplier Institute begins providing extensive training to automotive suppliers and other industries.

1987 Budd Company and Kelsey-Hayes — first case study outside of Japan.

Beginning of QFD training at Ford and General Motors.

1988 Utilization of QFD throughout the United States.

Harvard Business Review publishes an article on "The House of Quality" by J. Hauser and D. Clausing in the May-June 1988 edition.

A series of articles appears in the June 1988 issue of *Quality Progress* depicting the relationship of QFD to Policy Management, SPC, and Taguchi methods.

1989   First Joint ASI, ASQC, and GOAL/QPC QFD Symposium in Novi, Michigan.

George Washington University begins commercial telecasts on QFD.

Technicomp video series on QFD available.

Numerous QFD software packages available.

1990   GOAL/QPC endorses QFD/Capture™ software.

GOAL/QPC introduces advanced QFD concepts.

Productivity Press publishes Dr. Akao's text, *QFD: Integrating Customer Requirements Into Design*.

Second Annual Joint ASI, ASQC, and GOAL/QPC QFD Symposium in Novi, Michigan.

1991   GOAL/QPC publishes research report, *Quality Function Deployment: Advanced QFD Application Articles*. Includes advanced QFD topics:

- Dynamic customer requirements
- Customer conversion sheet
- Advanced Quality Function Deployment

Third Annual ASI, GOAL/QPC QFD Symposium in Novi, Michigan.

GOAL/QPC introduces an advanced QFD course.

Chapter 5

Overview of Quality Function Deployment

This chapter provides a set of visual aids that a facilitator or trainer can use for an overview presentation to introduce QFD to his or her organization. The facing page for each visual contains additional information that amplifies and highlights the bullets in each visual.

This is not intended to be an all-inclusive presentation and should be modified by facilitators or trainers based on their personal experiences within their organization. The result of the QFD Readiness Assessment constructed in Chapter 3 is an additional topic that can be covered during an overview presentation. The result of this assessment process can be used to show where QFD can initially be of most benefit to the organization. Some of the history of QFD in Chapter 4 may also be included in this overview presentation.

A Definition of Quality

The ability to meet or exceed customer expectations while maintaining a competitive market position.

Visual 1: Facilitator and Trainer Notes

A Definition of Quality

- The focus is on the customer's needs and expectations, not the organization's ability to produce. This is equally important for service and manufacturing organizations.

- The organization needs to understand what its basic business is, who its customers are, and what their needs and wants are.

- The organization needs to focus on cost, quality, and timeliness and thoroughly understand its market position.

A Definition of Quality

The ability to meet or exceed customer expectations while maintaining a competitive market position.

A Definition of QFD

A structured and disciplined process that provides a means to identify and carry the voice of the customer through each stage of product or service development and implementation.

QFD is:

- **Communication**
- **Documentation**
- **Analysis**
- **Prioritization** >breakthroughs

Visual 2: Facilitator and Trainer Notes

A Definition of QFD

- QFD is a structured and disciplined process that takes time.

- QFD uses customer input to develop, implement, and improve a product or service.

- QFD improves communication in the following ways:
  - The organization acts to understand its external customer.
  - Vertical departments are involved in the design and development of products and services.
  - QFD provides a team structure, which improves communication among team members.
  - The QFD team and management communicate in a structured, documented fashion.

- The QFD matrices provide a detailed project tracking system that incorporates the QFD team's consensus thinking process.

- The QFD matrices provide a structured approach to analyze and prioritize the input to the matrices.

A Definition of QFD

A structured and disciplined process that provides a means to identify and carry the voice of the customer through each stage of product or service development and implementation.

QFD is:

- Communication
- Documentation
- Analysis
- Prioritization $\rangle$ breakthroughs

Japanese QFD Results

- Design time was reduced by 1/3 to 1/2

- Problems with initial quality decreased

- Comparison and analysis of competitive products became possible

- Communication between divisions improved

Visual 3: Facilitator and Trainer Notes

Japanese QFD Results

- Design time was reduced by one-third to one-half based on a study by Yoji Akao for JUSE in 1978. Reference *Better Designs in Half the Time* by Bob King, page 1-3, edition 3.0.

- Companies using QFD found a decrease in product/service problems related to design because QFD focused the organization on capability-driven designs.

- Chart A-1, part 1 provides a section to benchmark the organization against its competitors based on the voice of the customer.

- Communication between organizational units improved because each organizational unit was a part of the QFD team and spoke based on facts and the voice of the customer.

Japanese QFD Results

- Design time was reduced by 1/3 to 1/2
- Problems with initial quality decreased
- Comparison and analysis of competitive products became possible
- Communication between divisions improved

Comparison of Old and New Design Systems

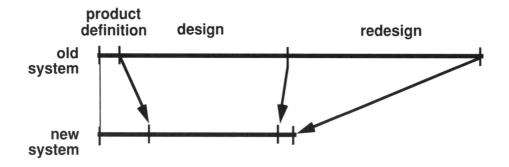

Visual 4: Facilitator and Trainer Notes

Comparison of Old and New Design Systems

- The old system created products with a design based on the voice of the engineer. It is often called "folklore" design because it is guided by intuition. The end result is products sent to manufacturing that do not meet process requirements, which causes continuous redesign and a wall placed between design and production and production and customer service. The method behind "folklore" design is "fire, ready, aim."

- The new system is based on a marketing approach that factually understands the customer's needs and expectations. By expanding the time taken to define the product, QFD virtually eliminates the need for redesign, especially on the critical items. Better documentation, improved communication, and a focus on priorities improves the efficiency of the initial design and significantly reduces the need for redesign.

Comparison of Old and New Design Systems

Organizing the QFD Project

- Decide upon the purpose
- Define the benefits
- Select the project
- Select the team

Visual 5: Facilitator and Trainer Notes

Organizing the QFD Project

- Management selects the product or service to be studied.

- The selection process is useful to:
  - Decide the purpose of the QFD study: is it a new design, an upgrade, or a cost reduction. This will establish the scope of the study.
  - Define the benefits that realistically should be achieved by the QFD project.
  - Select the products or services that have a high priority to the organization.
  - Identify team members who are decision makers and represent a variety of disciplines, such as research and development, engineering, finance, marketing, production, and customer service.

Organizing the QFD Project

- Decide upon the purpose
- Define the benefits
- Select the project
- Select the team

Describing the Product/Service

- **What new technology can be applied to obtain a product/service breakthrough?**

- **What are the costs involved?**

- **Are there different ways of fulfilling the purpose of the product or service?**

- **Are any of the key items bottlenecks?**

- **How might the product/service fail?**

Visual 6: Facilitator and Trainer Notes

Describing the Product/Service

- The descriptive phase of the QFD study involves understanding who the customer is and capturing in the customer's words the needs and expectations for the product or service. The Voice of the Customer Table, introduced in Chapter 8, expands on this topic.

- Progressing through the QFD charts takes us from a planning process through an acting process and determines how the customer wants will be fulfilled. Reference figures 9-1, 9-2, and 9-6.

- The purpose of the product or service is determined as we detail its functions. Reference Charts B-1 and A-2, described in Chapter 10.

- The sub-system level design process that deals with concepts is described. The prioritization of the concepts will then lead us to the methodology to accomplish them, as shown in figure 9-6.

Describing the Product/Service

- What new technology can be applied to obtain a product/service breakthrough?
- What are the costs involved?
- Are there different ways of fulfilling the purpose of the product or service?
- Are any of the key items bottlenecks?
- How might the product/service fail?

The Breakthrough Phase

Breakthroughs are activities that result in product or service improvement or bottleneck removal through an organized, structured process.

Visual 7: Facilitator and Trainer Notes

The Breakthrough Phase

The team identifies potential bottleneck or problem areas and analyzes them to identify feasible improvement solutions. Feasible solutions may include:
- New technology
- New functions
- New concepts
- Improved reliability
- Cost reduction
- Changed processes

QFD Overview: Visual 7

The Breakthrough Phase

Breakthroughs are activities that result in product or service improvement or bottleneck removal through an organized, structured process.

Implementation

The development of a total product or service plan that:

- Defines what the product/service is

- Describes the steps to be accomplished

- Defines the development and production requirements necessary to satisfy customer expectations

Visual 8: Facilitator and Trainer Notes

Implementation

The culmination of the QFD team process results in a complete descriptive product or service plan that identifies the elements shown on Visual 8. This is not a static plan but rather a dynamic one that must be reviewed continually focused on the following:

- Changes in the voice of the customer
- Advancements by competition
- Technological breakthroughs
- Improved support systems
- Availability of new materials or methods

Implementation

The development of a total product or service plan that:

- **Defines what the product/service is**
- **Describes the steps to be accomplished**
- **Defines the development and production requirements necessary to satisfy customer expectations**

In the United States

Generally QFD practitioners in the United States do not progress beyond Chart A-1. There are several reasons for this.

1. Chart A-1 tells you a lot so it is valuable by itself.

2. Many companies are doing large charts (100x100 items or 10,000 possible correlations), thus making it very time consuming.

3. Because of large A-1 charts, many do not have the energy or interest to go on to other charts.

4. Because QFD is relatively new, people are afraid to make a mistake and so they keep working on the A-1 chart.

5. Some are concerned that because of limited customer information, the results of the A-1 chart may be incorrect, so they are reluctant to take possible wrong conclusions to other charts.

Visual 9: Facilitator and Trainer Notes

In the United States

- Research by GOAL/QPC has indicated that many organizations using QFD stop after Chart A-1 for the reasons listed on Visual 9.

- To overcome the time-consuming process and difficulties noted, the Voice of the Customer Table, introduced in Chapter 8, helps to organize the customer input so it flows to the appropriate charts rather than being stuffed into Chart A-1.

In the United States

Generally QFD practitioners in the United States do not progress beyond Chart A-1. There are several reasons for this.

1. Chart A-1 tells you a lot so it is valuable by itself.

2. Many companies are doing large charts (100x100 items or 10,000 possible correlations), thus making it very time consuming.

3. Because of large A-1 charts, many do not have the energy or interest to go on to other charts.

4. Because QFD is relatively new, people are afraid to make a mistake and so they keep working on the A-1 chart.

5. Some are concerned that because of limited customer information, the results of the A-1 chart may be incorrect, so they are reluctant to take possible wrong conclusions to other charts.

Lessons from Successful QFD Applications

1. Using the Voice of the Customer Table keeps the chart size manageable.

2. Manageable chart size reduces the time barrier most teams encounter.

3. Manageable charts, reduced time, and correct QFD application encourages QFD teams to gravitate to other important matrices.

Visual 10: Facilitator and Trainer Notes

Lessons from Successful QFD Applications

The Voice of the Customer Table helps overcome the difficulties shown in Visual 9 and keeps chart sizes manageable. In the past, functions, cost, quality characteristics, and reliability items were often included in customer demands, thus lengthening and confusing the process.

Lessons from Successful QFD Applications

1. Using the Voice of the Customer Table keeps the chart size manageable.

2. Manageable chart size reduces the time barrier most teams encounter.

3. Manageable charts, reduced time, and correct QFD application encourages QFD teams to gravitate to other important matrices.

Chapter 6

Lessons to be Learned

The Quality Function Deployment facilitation process is one of constant learning and continuous improvement. The lessons presented in this chapter will assist those just starting out or recently involved in the training and facilitation of QFD. The lessons include a list of potential pitfalls to be aware of and to prepare for during the implementation process.

Lesson Number 1: Cultural Requirements

For QFD to be successful in any organization, a change has to take place in the organization's culture and in the way day-to-day business is conducted. QFD requires a mindset change in all departments from a reactive to a proactive approach to problem solving. Problems and bottlenecks must be anticipated and corrected during design rather than during production.

Lesson Number 2: Faddish

It is not unusual for management to adopt the latest fad to look good. QFD is no exception to this rule and if it is adopted just for show, failure is inevitable. QFD will succeed only if top management is totally committed to the process. It must also be accepted completely by the organizations using it.

Lesson Number 3: Projects for Study

Choose initial projects carefully. It is best to start small and then go for bigger projects.

Starting small allows for experimentation with the QFD process. Also, implementing QFD is not as simple as some literature suggests, because in addition to the QFD process, you have to contend with the human interactions that take place. Go after the heavy hitters once you have first felt your way through a few small projects.

Lesson Number 4: An Advocator Versus a Doer

An advocator is not necessarily a doer. It is easy for program managers to advocate the QFD process and not get involved. Program managers cannot delegate their leadership responsibility to other members of the program team; they must be active leaders of the QFD study. If the program manager does not show full commitment to the process then why should the rest of the program management team show commitment?

Lesson Number 5: Program Manager Involvement

The program manager must support and be committed to the QFD process and develop an atmosphere that encourages openness, new ideas, and risk taking. The program manager must work with the participants to develop reasonable expectations of what this process will do to help the ultimate design and fabrication of the product under study.

Lesson Number 6: Selecting the QFD Team

The team members for any QFD study should be the decision makers in the organization. The team should have representatives from marketing, research, engineering, manufacturing, and the program management team. It is important to spend the time to recruit the top individuals from these functions. This will enhance the output of the study and ensure top level "buy-in" to the results and actions that must be taken.

Lesson Number 7: Commitment

The QFD team members must commit to the process by being on time for and attending all sessions. They must commit 100 percent or not at all. Lukewarm participation is detrimental to the success of the study.

Lesson Number 8: Training

How to train personnel in the fundamentals of QFD is a question that needs to be addressed carefully. Mass training does not usually work well. Participants of mass training quickly forget what they have learned if it is not applied soon after the training. On-the-project training is often successful because the team participants learn the principles of QFD together and apply them immediately to their own projects rather than to a fabricated training example.

Lesson Number 9: What Do We Use the QFD Meetings For?

The QFD meeting should be for updating the charts and the team members. The member assignments must be completed between meetings and not during the meeting. The leader must not let unprepared members sidetrack the group's efforts.

Lesson Number 10: What to Tell the QFD Participants

The start of a QFD study is the time to tell the team members honestly what they are in for. A QFD study is a trying, tedious, and time-consuming process.

Lesson Number 11: Benefits of QFD

The main benefit of a completed QFD study is that it helps to create a common group vision of what the product should be and where in the development/design stage it is now.

Lesson Number 12: When to Do the QFD Study

The QFD study should be done as early in the design stage as possible. If the design is almost complete, it is too late to get the potential participants in the study to accept any creative changes because their focus will already be on getting the product to market.

Lesson Number 13: Is QFD a Savior?

QFD is not a savior for projects in trouble — it is a devil. A QFD study on a program in trouble will only magnify its flaws.

Lesson Number 14: QFD Usages

QFD is not limited to products sold externally. It can be used internally for organizational studies, training assessments, internal services, departments supplying each other with products, vendor/vendee relationships, etc. QFD is a useful tool for improving group thinking around any organizational situation.

Lesson Number 15: Obtaining the Voice of the Customer

This is the drive shaft of the QFD engine. Without an accurate and detailed understanding of the voice of the customer, there can be no study. This is the most important and the most time-consuming step of the entire process. Much has been written about the various ways to obtain the voice of the customer, from formal to informal methods. The study group should consult the marketing research department as to the best methods for its study. The group should also confirm what it determines to be the voice of the customer with follow-up interviews or surveys.

Lesson Number 16: Implosion or Explosion of the Voice of the Customer

If the QFD study group decides to brainstorm what it initially feels the voice of the customer is, the group can use the Affinity Diagram approach of organizing the customer's needs into primary, secondary, and tertiary categories. A useful method for a group that is having trouble generating the customer's wants is the reverse of the previous methods. Instead of "exploding out" the customer's needs, the group implodes them. The program manager lists seven key phrases of the project and from this tertiary list the secondary and primary categories are developed. Then the entire listing is reviewed for completeness and given a reality check with market research.

Lesson Number 17: Are Silent Conversations Useful?

The silent group conversations take place when you use the Affinity Diagram. This silent movement of the pieces of the Affinity Diagram into logical clusters is a useful method to draw out reticent group members and allow them an opportunity to display their feelings and thinking to the group. Often after this exercise they feel more comfortable and express their ideas more openly.

Lesson Number 18: How Many Customers are There?

Often during the process of obtaining the voice of the customer, potential users other than the primary customer emerge. For instance, the person who purchases the product is interested in price and delivery while the ultimate user could be interested in the controls, speed, "up time," size, color, etc. Look for all potential customers during the search for the voice of the customer.

Lesson Number 19: Beliefs and Experience

A common reaction to a completed QFD study by those who did not participate in the study is "The customer is wrong." If the QFD study obtains an accurate assessment of the voice of the customer, it is not unusual for those who design and build the products to disagree with it. It conflicts with their beliefs and experience, therefore they do not easily accept the data.

Lesson Number 20: Subdivide and Conquer

Once the voice of the customer has been obtained and agreed upon by the study group, the remainder of Chart A-1 ("House of Quality") can be subdivided and assigned to subgroups of the team. This will cut down on the amount of time needed to complete the study. The subgroups work independently and develop a trial balloon of their section for review with the total group. This approach is suggested only for a group that has done a study previously and understands the total process.

Lesson Number 21: What Is the Right Approach?

A QFD study can vary from simple to sophisticated depending on the output desired.

There are many variations (additions) that can be made to Chart A-1. In essence there is no one right approach. The approach chosen must fit the circumstances.

Lesson Number 22: Varying Benefits of QFD

The stage of development at which the QFD study is conducted will determine the benefits derived. If the study is conducted early in the design process the benefits can include:
- Team building
- Determining who the customers are
- Focusing the design
- Positioning the marketing strategy

If the study is done later in the design process the benefits can include:
- Confirmation of beliefs
- Bringing everyone to the same knowledge level
- Focusing on the work to be done
- Identifying what can be done on the design and what cannot

Lesson Number 23: Are We Having Fun Yet?

It is the responsibility of the leader and/or facilitator to keep the group's spirits up during the study. It is easy for the team to get bogged down in trivial detail and lose the "big picture" of the study. It is a good practice at the end of each session to do a reality check with the participants. This gives them a chance to express their feelings. Sometimes minor logistical items can be big dissatisfiers and may never get mentioned. Attention to the working rules of the meetings is essential to keep the process functioning smoothly.

Lesson Number 24: Chart Development

A lot of learning occurs within the group during the development of the QFD study

chart(s). It is best to have the group develop the chart and not delegate it to the facilitator.

Lesson Number 25: Plan Values Are Not Specifications (in Chart A-1)

One point should be reinforced (especially to designers and engineers in the group): the plan values are not specifications. They are what the customer wants. This is easily confused. The plan values are the values that satisfy the customer and not what is necessarily currently obtainable. They are targets to strive for and around which tradeoffs are made.

Lesson Number 26: QFD Breaks the Established Design Cycle

Design, redesign, recall, and rework are all too familiar in the design of new products. QFD can help break this cycle by preventing defects in the design stage, rather than "fire-fighting" them in manufacturing.

Lesson Number 27: Fire Fighters Versus Preventers

QFD is resisted because it is logical and preaches the prevention of defects. The people who resist it are those who fix rather than prevent problems.

Lesson Number 28: Doubters and Detractors May Look Right in the End

When a QFD study is completed, do not be surprised by the following comments:
- It took you how long to produce that chart?
- Why didn't you ask me? I could have told you that.

To those who did not participate, the completed study looks easy and the entries on the chart may seem obvious. Non-participants cannot see the team work, consensus building, and level of trust developed during the production of the very accurate document.

Lesson Number 29: Continuous Improvement

QFD is a process and should be subjected to review and continuous improvement. Users of QFD should be constantly looking for better ways to use this tool in their organizations.

Lesson Number 30: Resistance

If you find that QFD is being resisted by various organizations, check on the following:
• The yawn quotient: Is the interest level low?
• Turf rumbles: Do not do it in my area, but I will help you implement it in other areas.
• Discipline aversion: The process is too strict; I cannot do it my way.

Lesson Number 31: A Questioning Process

QFD makes us question all of our actions and reasons for developing or modifying a product or service. It forces us away from myopic thought processes and fosters a broad point of view.

Lesson Number 32: Software

There are a number of software packages available to help with the tedious work of chart preparation. QFD software is recommended for mature QFD teams who are experienced with the process. ITI's QFD/Capture™ software is recommended because of its ease of use and flexibility. However, a team can learn a lot by doing the charts manually at first.

Lesson Number 33: Accept the Truth

There is no magic in QFD, only hard work and attention to details. The major goal is to elicit and listen to the voice of the customer.

Lesson Number 34: Go Back to Lesson Number 1

No matter how many times you use QFD it is always a good idea to review the past pitfalls and be wary of history repeating itself.

These lessons are related to Chart A-1 and the cultural requirements necessary for successful introduction and implementation of Quality Function Deployment. However, these lessons are applicable to all the other Quality Function Deployment charts as well.

Chapter 7

The Wallace Wallet Works Case Study

The Wallace Wallet Works is a fictitious corporation. It is presented here as an interactive group problem-solving exercise in which Quality Function Deployment is used to develop a new product.

This case study allows the participants to focus on the Quality Function Deployment process and tools and minimizes the emotional involvement that groups experience when they use the QFD process on a real issue. The facilitator should mention at the beginning to the participants that the primary focus of this exercise is "hands-on" experience with the process and tools. Emphasize that participants should concentrate in their group work on using the QFD process and should not become emotionally involved in a solution.

There are many possible solutions to this case study depending upon the market segment chosen. The facilitator should take advantage of the different solutions during a group review to highlight the importance of understanding the customer(s) before starting a QFD study.

This case study and group participative activities have the following benefits to the participants:
- Reinforcement of lecture material.
- Actual practice with the QFD tools and matrices.
- Team building.

Having everyone show their wallet starts a process of disclosure about who each of the participants is. The facilitator must be careful to keep the groups on track with the exercises spelled out in the case study. Groups sometimes enjoy comparing wallets and lose track of the objective of the exercise.

The Wallace Wallet Works case study is a self-contained exercise with all the necessary forms provided in the appendix.

A completed QFD analysis is developed in the succeeding chapters.

QFD

QUALITY FUNCTION DEPLOYMENT

CASE STUDY:

"THE WALLACE WALLET WORKS"

The Wallace Wallet Works:
A QFD Case Study

The Wallace Wallet Works is a one-product company founded in 1930. Its product is a plastic wallet with a snap change pocket, five inches by five and a half inches when folded. The front of the wallet is imprinted with the faces of popular children's characters or actors.

The company's annual sales last year were 18 million dollars. The company has consistently maintained a ten-percent profit margin. All sales are currently made in the United States. The company is located in Massachusetts in its own 50,000 square foot manufacturing plant and has 500 employees.

History

1930	Founded by William Wilhelm Wallace
1930s	Gene Autry Wallets
1940s	Roy Rogers Wallets
1950s	Elvis Wallets
1960s	Beatles Wallets
1970s	Flintstone Wallets
1980s	Ronald Reagan Wallets
1989	Batman Wallets
1990	Bart Simpson Wallets
1991	Desert Storm Camouflage Wallets

Case Problem

The new president of the Wallace Wallet Works, Wilamena Wilbur Wallace, is concerned that foreign competition is slowly eroding the company's market share by producing unlicensed copies of its products.

The company recently completed a five-year business plan with a goal of expanding from a one-product to a multi-product line. The plan is to expand sales by attracting new customers and by penetrating foreign markets.

The company wants to develop a new wallet that will appeal to adults in both the United States and foreign markets. The marketing department has developed a product requirement document outlining what this new wallet should be like.

Product Requirement: New Adult Wallet

- World class.
- Appealing to both men and women.
- Easily carried.
- Provides ample storage.
- Compact.
- Attractive.
- Durable.
- Rugged.
- Small size.
- Constructed of leather or another high-quality material.

Assignment

The Wallace Wallet Works has selected your team to provide Quality Function Deployment consulting services to help develop the new product. Your team has agreed as a first phase to develop Chart A-1 detailing the following:

1. **Voice of the Customer**
   - Identify who the potential customers are.
   - Brainstorm the voice of the customer.
   - Use the customer's language.
   - Try for positive and complete statements.

- No one-word statements.
- Arrange using an Affinity Diagram.
- Screen the arranged data to be sure it represents the voice of the customer. Remove any functions, quality characteristics, etc., and replace with demanded quality items. Use the attached QFD Voice of the Customer Table as a guide (Attachments 7-1 and 7-2).
- Analyze the demanded quality items to two levels in a Tree Diagram (four to five header cards with four to five second-level items).

2. Rank the Customer Demanded Quality
- Provide a ranking for each of the second level of detail demanded quality items on a scale of one (low) to three (medium) to five (high) for its importance. Use the levels two and four as compromises to reach consensus.

3. Company Now and Competitive Analysis
- Use the wallets of each person in your team for this step.
  - The worst-looking wallet in the group is the company's product now. This is the way the product is coming off the assembly line today.
  - Establish a rating for the "company now wallet" versus each of the second-level demanded quality items using the same scale that was used in the customer importance ratings.
  - The two best-looking wallets represent your competition. Develop a rating for each of these versus the demanded quality items using the same scale.

4. Company Plan
- For each second-level demanded quality item, determine where the company

should be in the future. Take into account the company's strategic plan, where the competition is, and the level of importance to the customer.

5. Ratio of Improvement
- Divide the company plan rating by the company now rating.

6. Sales Point
- Review the company plan rating versus its corresponding demanded quality to determine its sales point. A strong sales point (1.5) would be exciting quality that the customer would be delighted with and buy. A medium sales point (1.2) would be something that might intrigue the customer, but not cause compulsive buying.
- All other sales points are given a value of 1.0 and are referred to as ho-hum sales points.

7. Calculate the Absolute Weight
- Multiply the rating of importance by the rate of improvement by the sales point. Then sum the resultants down the column. This process step allows us to factor into the voice of the customer the company's improvement plans plus our indicators of marketing advantage. This composite score is more inclusive of key demanded quality items than just using the voice of the customer alone.

8. Demand Weight
- Divide the absolute weight column total into each individual item in the column and convert to a percentage. Identify the top three to five demanded quality items.

9. Quality Characteristics
- Quality characteristics are measurable items that ensure demanded quality is met.

- Arrange them into a three-level Tree Diagram.
- Pick ten items from the third level of the tree to be used in the matrix.
- Develop through brainstorming a list of quality characteristics.
- Remember that quality characteristics are measurable items.
- Avoid specifying test parameters. Instead, use the test purpose.

10. **Relationships**
- Develop the relationship matrix between the demanded quality items and the quality characteristics.
- Use the following relationships:

    ◎ = 9 (strong relationship)

    ○ = 3 (medium relationship)

    △ = 1 (possible or weak relationship)

- Do not force relationships.
- Multiply each relationship value by the corresponding demanded weights and record them in that cell.
- Sum each column and then total each of the sums.
- Change each column sum to a percentage.
- Identify the top three to five quality characteristics.

The entire QFD case study must be completed in three hours, including your presentation to the Wallace Wallet Works management. The Wallace Wallet Works is committed to this concept of new product development. To show its commitment the company has agreed to have a representative available for consultation throughout the case study for clarification. The representative is John Wallace Moran, Jr. (great-grandson of the founder) or your instructor (a distant cousin). Feel free to call upon the company representative at any time during the case study.

Attachments

Attachment 7-1:
    Voice of the Customer Table, Part 1 (reference Chapter 8)

Attachment 7-2:
    Voice of the Customer Table, Part 2 (reference Chapter 8)

Attachment 7-3:
    Chart A-1

Attachment 7-4:
    Generic Quality Table

Attachment 7-5:
    Definitions

I.D.	Customer Characteristics (who)		Voice of the Customer	Use											
				what		when		where		why		how			
	I/E	Data		I/E	Data	I/E	Data	I/E	Data	I/E	Data	I/E	Data		

Attachment 7-1 Voice of the Customer Table, Part 1

Reworded Data	Demanded Quality	Quality Characteristics	Function	Reliability	Comments

Attachment 7-2 Voice of the Customer Table, Part 2

Quality Characteristics

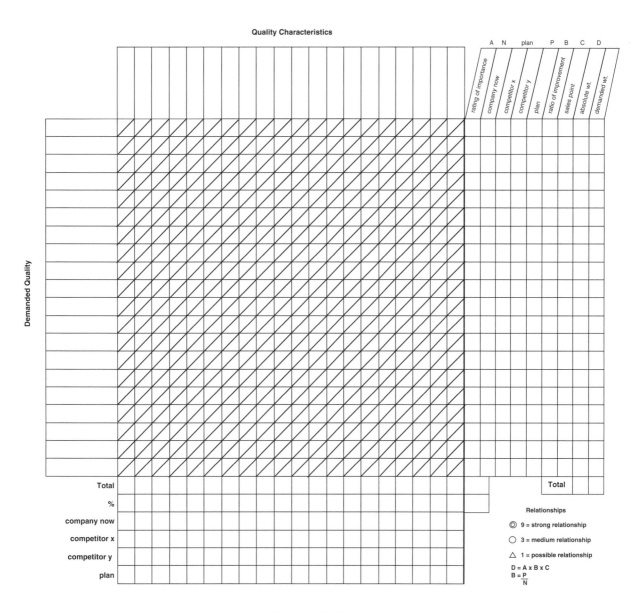

Attachment 7-3 Chart A-1

Quality Characteristics

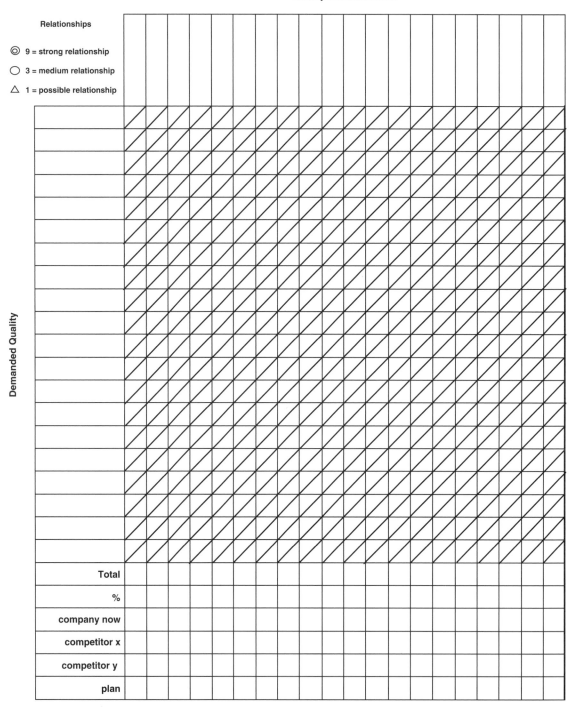

Relationships

◎ 9 = strong relationship

○ 3 = medium relationship

△ 1 = possible relationship

Demanded Quality

Total

%

company now

competitor x

competitor y

plan

Attachment 7-4 Generic Quality Table

Attachment 7-5: QFD Definitions

Demanded Quality

A transformation of the voice of the customer into statements that are understandable by the organization.

Quality Characteristic

A measurable item that ensures demanded quality items will be met.

Functions

Tasks that are necessary for the product or service to be deliverable and acceptable to the customer. A statement expressing function should contain an active verb and an object (noun).

Concept

A method for achieving functions (enabling tasks).

Element

An item needed for achieving the best concepts.

Chapter 8

Understanding the Voice of the Customer

The most difficult part of any QFD study is obtaining a complete and accurate voice of the customer. Using a Cause and Effect Diagram is one approach a facilitator or trainer could take in an overview or training session on QFD to illustrate the complexity of gathering a complete and accurate voice of the customer.

Figure 8-1 shows the major causal factors involved in obtaining the voice of the customer.

These causal factors are:
- Who is the customer?
- How is the voice of the customer heard?
- How is the voice of the customer evaluated?
- Who is responsible for keeping an accurate voice of the customer?

Other causal factors may be added that are specific to your organization or industry.

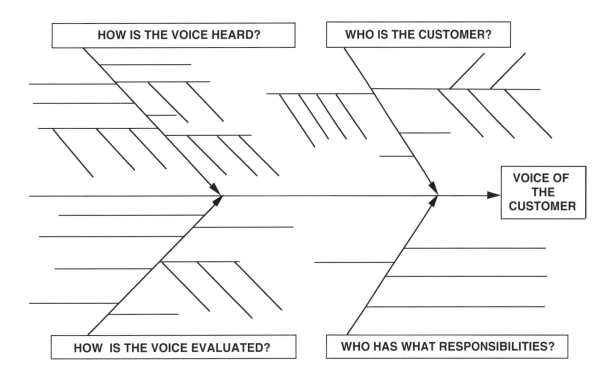

Figure 8-1. Cause and Effect Diagram

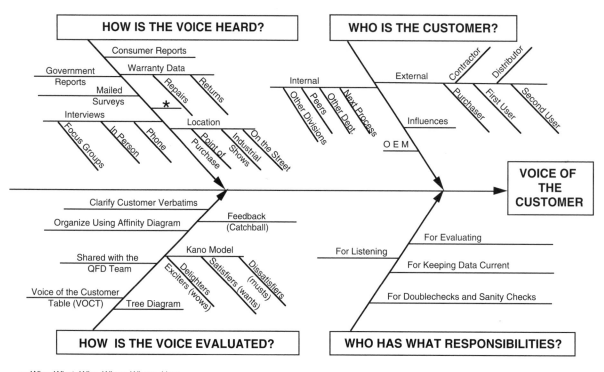

HOW IS THE VOICE HEARD?

Consumer Reports
Warranty Data
Government Reports
Mailed Surveys
Interviews
Focus Groups
In Person
Phone
Repairs
★
Returns
Point of Purchase
Industrial Shows
On the Street
Location

WHO IS THE CUSTOMER?

Internal
Other Divisions
Peers
Other Dept.
Next Process
External
Contractor
Distributor
Purchaser
First User
Second User
Influences
O E M

VOICE OF THE CUSTOMER

Clarify Customer Verbatims
Organize Using Affinity Diagram
Feedback (Catchball)
Shared with the QFD Team
Kano Model
Delighters Exciters (wows)
Satisfiers (wants)
Dissatisfiers (musts)
Voice of the Customer Table (VOCT)
Tree Diagram

For Listening
For Evaluating
For Keeping Data Current
For Doublechecks and Sanity Checks

HOW IS THE VOICE EVALUATED?

WHO HAS WHAT RESPONSIBILITIES?

★ Who, What, Why, When, Where, How

Figure 8-2. Example of a Completed Cause and Effect Diagram for Obtaining the Voice of the Customer

Figure 8-2 shows an example of a completed Cause and Effect Diagram for obtaining the voice of the customer.

A facilitator or trainer can use the Cause and Effect Diagram to explore the complexity and difficulty of capturing and understanding the voice of the customer. First, the facilitator or trainer can ask the participants for ideas to fill in the blank Cause and Effect Diagram as shown in figure 8-1. Next, the facilitator or trainer should ask the participants to vote on which entries in the Cause and Effect Diagram they are doing today in their organization. After the voting has taken place, the participants should vote on how effectively each of the items being done today captures the voice of their customer and communicates it throughout their organization.

These interactive exercises ensure that the participants have an opportunity to discuss and appreciate the complexity of the task, the organization's current approaches, the effectiveness of these approaches, and the difficulty in keeping the voice of the customer current. The facilitator or trainer should now introduce the Voice of the Customer Table (VOCT), part 1 as shown in figure 8-3 and part 2 as shown in figure 8-4.

I.D.	Customer Characteristics (who)		Voice of the Customer	Use											
				what		when		where		why		how			
	I/E	Data		I/E	Data	I/E	Data	I/E	Data	I/E	Data	I/E	Data		

Figure 8-3. Voice of the Customer Table, Part 1

Reworded Data	Demanded Quality	Quality Characteristics	Function	Reliability	Comments

Figure 8-4. Voice of the Customer Table, Part 2

The VOCT is a technique to organize, analyze, and profile the customer and his or her use of the product or service being provided. The VOCT is a way to gain an in-depth understanding of customers and their needs and is divided into the following sections:

Voice of the Customer Table, Part 1

I.D.: Identification number. This is used to reference a particular set of characteristics.

I/E: Source of data, internal or external.

Data:
- Type of customer. General categories (male/female, etc.).
- Particular types of customer under each category.

Voice of customer
Use for the product or service (present or planned):
- What
- When
- Where
- Why
- How

Voice of the Customer Table, Part 2

Reworded data
A process of extracting all possible demands that a customer may include in a statement of wants and needs. The multiple demands contained in the customer words are singularized via the rewording activity. This process also includes the analysis of usage.

Demanded quality
A transformation of the voice of the customer (including reworded data) into statements that are understandable by the development organization.

Quality characteristics
Measurable items that ensure demanded quality items are met.

Functions
Tasks that are necessary for the product or service to be deliverable and acceptable to the customer. They constitute what the product or service does.

Reliability
The likelihood that a product or service will satisfy its intended purpose for a specified time period.

Comments
Statements that are important to carry forward in the project but don't fit any predefined column in the VOCT.

The columns shown here as being part of the Voice of the Customer Table, parts 1 and 2, are those that are used the most. The facilitator or trainer may add other columns such as cost or safety depending on the needs of the organization, project, or application.

In this section only part 1 of Voice of the Customer Table will be discussed. Part 2 of the Voice of the Customer Table will be deferred to the next chapter.

The facilitator or trainer can use the following suggested prompts to explain each section of the Voice of the Customer Table.

SECTION	PROMPT
Who will be using the product?	• type of customer • expertise level • gender • sex • educational level
What will the product be used for?	• purpose for buying • need fulfilled • primary use • secondary use
When will it be used?	• time of year • season of year • frequency of use
Where will it be used?	• geographic location • operating conditions • environmental extremes
Why is it being used?	• special properties required • safety concerns • customized needs
How will it be used?	• operating procedures • continually or occasionally • industrial use • consumer use

The Voice of the Customer Table directs the QFD team to gaps in its understanding of the customer's expectations. In addition, it requires a QFD team to fully understand how the customer plans to use the product or service. The gaps identified in either part of the Voice of the Customer Table are action items on which the QFD team must follow-up. The action items may require the team to seek expertise outside of the group to help complete the analysis.

Figure 8-5 shows the Wallace Wallet Works case study solution flow. Figures 8-6 and 8-7 show examples of parts 1 and 2 of the Voice of the Customer Table for the Wallace Wallet Works.

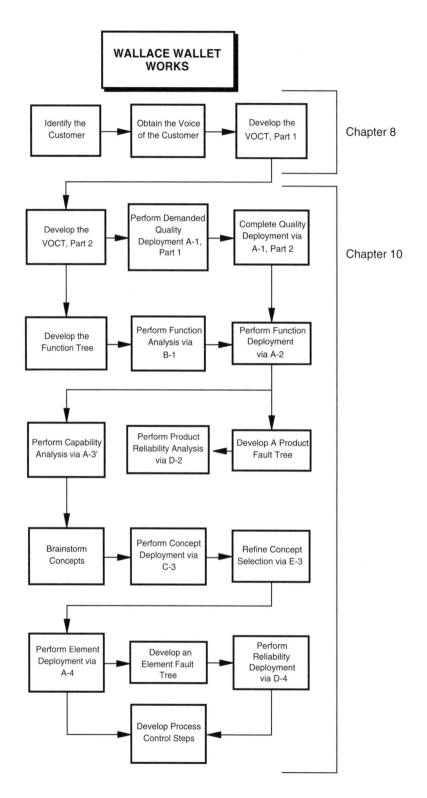

Figure 8-5. Wallace Wallet Works Case Study Solution Flow

I.D.	Customer Characteristics (who)		Voice of the Customer	Use									
				what		when		where		why		how	
	I/E	Data		I/E	Data	I/E	Data	I/E	Data	I/E	Data	I/E	Data
1.	E	Male, 26 years old	Wallet feels smooth			I	I take it from pocket	E	In my hand				
2.			It's easy to remove					I	In my pocket				
3.			I have easy access to cards	E	Credit cards License					I	Sometimes in a hurry	I	Via pockets
4.	E	Female, 35 years old	I can carry money			I	I am out shopping	I	In my purse In my pocket	I	Conceal my money		
5.			I can carry credit cards when shopping			E	When I am shopping	I	Stores Entertainment Restaurants	I	Don't have to carry money	I	Clear plastic
6.			I want contents visible			I	I need fast access	I	Banks Gas stations Stores	I	In a hurry		

Figure 8-6. Wallace Wallet Works Voice of the Customer Table, Part 1

I.D.	Customer Characteristics (who)		Voice of the Customer	Use									
				what		when		where		why		how	
	I/E	Data		I/E	Data	I/E	Data	I/E	Data	I/E	Data	I/E	Data
7.	E	Female, 43 years old	I want to carry many items	I	Pictures Letters	I	I go shopping I visit friends	I	Stores	I	Don't need other carriers		
8.			I want it to last a long time							I	I like the one I have		
9.			I don't want to spend a lot of money							I	Would use money for other things	I	
10.		Female, 35 years old	It makes me feel important	I	Status Symbol	I	I display it	I	My friends are pleased	I	I like the feeling	I	Clear plastic

Figure 8-7. Wallace Wallet Works Voice of the Customer Table, Part 2

A facilitator or trainer can begin the Wallace Wallet Works case study by dividing the participants into groups of five to eight members and having them fill out the Voice of the Customer Table, part 1 for the wallet. This exercise will help the group focus on the market segment it intends to target with this wallet. The groups should be allowed 30-45 minutes to complete this exercise. The facilitator should then have the groups report on their findings. The facilitator should prepare, in advance, a Voice of the Customer Table, part 1 on a few sheets of flip chart paper and should fill it in as the groups report, capturing all the ideas generated.

Another option is to have the groups write their ideas on the master Voice of the Customer flip chart in different colors. The groups can put a check mark next to those ideas already on the chart to indicate a similar idea. The different colors will show the diversity of ideas generated and will highlight that a QFD team needs to solicit ideas from a wide range of individuals and functions, both internal and external to the organization, to develop a complete Voice of the Customer Table.

Chapter 9

Matrix of Matrices Flow: The Tool Box

A common question posed to facilitators or trainers from QFD teams or training participants is "After Chart A-1, where do we go next? A-2? A-3? B-1? E-4?" The question of which chart to proceed to after Chart A-1 is not an easy one to answer. When we posed this question to one of our co-authors, Satoshi Nakui, he gave us the following two answers: "Case by case." and "It depends."

At first we did not appreciate his answers since they were not very explicit. We realized later, however, that these are the appropriate responses to the question of which chart next. Each QFD study has different characteristics and purposes for which it is undertaken. The chart to proceed to after Chart A-1 depends on the scope and objectives of the QFD study.

This chapter will cover a series of possible flows through the Matrix of Matrices, as shown in figure 9-1. These flows will each assume a stated purpose for a QFD study and can be used as a general guideline for those using charts beyond Chart A-1. These flows can be modified or rearranged to achieve the stated purpose of your QFD study. There are many possible flows through the Matrix of Matrices. This chapter illustrates the most frequently used, which cover the following:

- Market Planning Design
- System Level Design
- Subsystem Level Design
- Element Level Design

This chapter will assume the reader is familiar with the contents of the matrices illustrated in this chapter. For more information on a specific matrix, refer to *Better Designs in Half the Time*, by Bob King, GOAL/QPC, 1989.

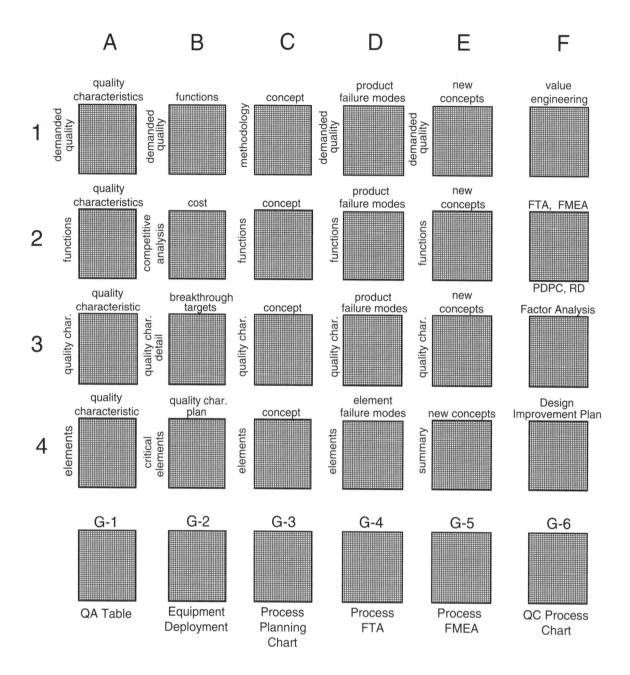

The Matrix of Matrices

From *Better Designs in Half the Time*, by Bob King, GOAL/QPC, © 1989.

Figure 9-1. Matrix of Matrices

Voice of the Customer Analysis

The analysis of the voice of the customer, shown in figure 9-2, is a process that gathers information from the customer and classifies it into categories. During this process we attempt to uncover demands that the customer has not told us about. These unspoken demands are then probed in detail.

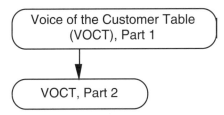

Figure 9-2. Analysis of the Voice of the Customer

Market Planning Flow

This process uses the Voice of the Customer Table and has two parts (see figures 8-3 and 8-4). The VOCT was first introduced as a customer voice conversion sheet in Japan[1].

This tool was Americanized by Satoshi Nakui and Stanley Marsh of GOAL/QPC. Chapter 8 provides a detailed explanation of this concept.

The next three design flows refer to additional charts in the matrix of matrices (see figure 9-1).

System Level Design Flow

The system level design process, shown in figure 9-3, consists of demanded quality deployment (Chart A-1), function deployment (Charts B-1 and A-2), reliability deployment (Charts D-1 and D-2), and part of capability deployment (Chart C-1'/C-1").

The components of the system level design process consist of the following deployments:

Demanded Quality Deployment (Chart A-1)
Demanded quality deployment is a process

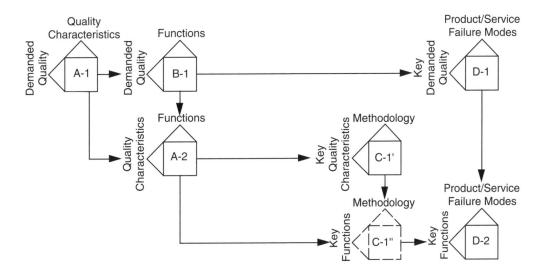

Figure 9-3. System Level Design Process

---

[1] *A Study on Writing Expressions of Demanded Quality,* Tadashi Ohfuji and Michiteru Ono, Japan Society of Quality Control (JSQC), 1990.

that identifies the relationships between demanded quality items and quality characteristics and converts the degree of importance for demanded quality into the degree of importance for quality characteristics. A plan for quality of new product or service and design target values of the important quality characteristics are also determined during this deployment activity.

Function Deployment (Chart B-1, A-2)
Function deployment is a process that identifies the tasks necessary to meet demanded quality, and identifies the relationships between functions, demanded quality items, and quality characteristics. It converts the degree of importance for each demanded quality item and quality characteristic to the degree of importance for each function.

Capability Deployment (Chart C-1', C-1")
Capability is defined as factors (such as methodology, failure mode, cost, and safety) that must be successfully met in new product or service development.

Reliability Deployment (Chart D-1, D-2 optional)
These two charts, although optional, provide a process that describes failure modes for a product or service based upon demanded quality or function, and identifies the associated relationships to help identify failure modes to be carried forward into further analysis.

Subsystem Level Design Flow

Subsystem level design, shown in figure 9-4, consists of concept deployment (Charts C-3 and E-3) and the completion of capability deployment (Charts C-1 and D-2'). Capability deployment was determined under system level design.

Methodology, shown in Chart C-1, may be defined as the techniques we possess or need in order to produce our product or service.

Chart C-1 identifies methodologies needed to achieve the key concepts. C-1 can be divided into C-1' in which we look at the relationship between methodology and key quality characteristics and C-1', which compares key functions to methodology. This relationship is shown in figure 9-4.

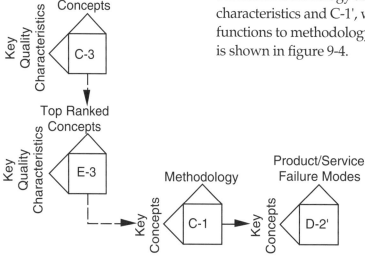

Figure 9-4. Subsystem Level Design

Chart C-1' describes the relationships between quality characteristic target values and the methodology for identifying or the capability to meet the planned targets.

Chart D-2' identifies the relationships between potential product/service failure modes and proposed key concepts.

Concept Deployment (Chart C-3)
A concept is a method for achieving functions (enabling tasks). The concepts, therefore, are based on functions. Concept deployment is a process that defines alternatives for achieving functions.

Element Level Design Flow

This section consists of element deployment (Chart A-4) and element failure mode deployment (Chart D-4) as shown in figure 9-5.

Element Deployment (Chart A-4)
An element is an item needed for achieving the best concepts. Element deployment is a process that extracts items needed for achieving concepts, and identifies the relationships between quality characteristics and these items.

Element Failure Mode Deployment (Chart D-4)
Element failure mode deployment is a process that identifies the relationships between elements and their failure modes (Chart D-4).

Figure 9-6 shows an overall integration of the four different design flows.

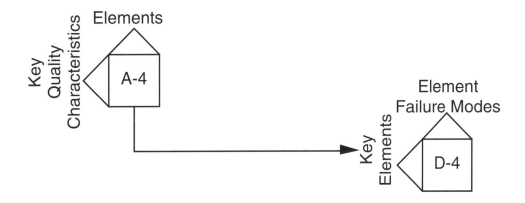

Figure 9-5. Element Level Design Flow

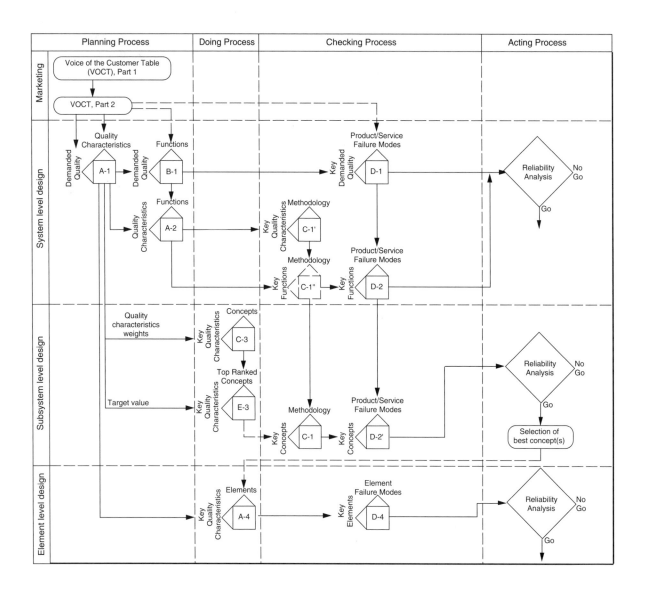

Figure 9-6. Integration of All Four Design Flows

Chapter 10

Wallace Wallet Works Case Study

This chapter is devoted to developing a QFD solution to the Wallace Wallet Works case study. This solution can help explain how Quality Function Deployment uses the voice of the customer to develop a product or service that meets or exceeds the needs and expectations of that customer. The solution developed in this chapter uses a sampling of the basic flow of the matrices shown in Chapter 9.

Figure 10-1 shows the Wallace Wallet Works case study solution flow.

This chapter's solution to the Wallace Wallet Works case study contains the following matrices:
- Voice of the Customer Table, part 1
- Chart A-1
- Chart B-1
- Chart A-2
- Chart D-2
- Chart C-3
- Chart E-3
- Chart A-3'
- Chart A-4
- Chart D-4
- Voice of the Customer Table, part 2

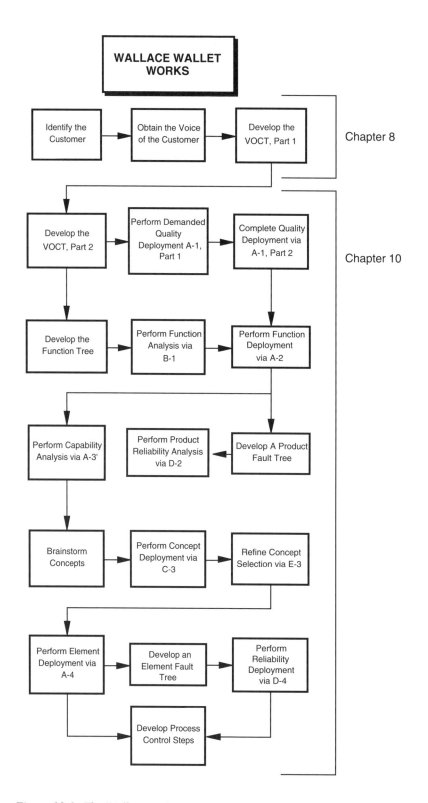

Figure 10-1. The Wallace Wallet Works Case Study Solution Flow

In part 2 of the Voice of the Customer Table (figure 8-4), the QFD team begins to sort the voice of the customer into the following categories:
- Demanded Quality
- Quality Characteristics
- Functions
- Reliability

The following is a possible list of customer demands generated through a brainstorming session with a team applying QFD to the Wallace Wallet Works case study to design a new adult wallet.

Brainstorming List of Customer Demands: Adult Wallet
1. Wallet feels smooth
2. It is easy to remove
3. I have easy access to cards
4. I can carry money
5. I can carry credit cards while shopping
6. I want contents visible
7. I want to carry many items
8. I want it to last a long time
9. I don't want to spend a lot of money for it
10. I want to calculate my checkbook balance

These brainstorming items are entered into the voice of the customer column in part 1 (figure 8-3) of the table and then we expand on these meanings in the reworded data column in part 2 of the table as shown in figure 10-2.

Now that the market planning flow is complete, we will begin the design phase of QFD. The matrices developed in the rest of this chapter illustrate the most frequently used charts described in Chapter 9. These charts illustrate the systems level, conceptual level, and element level design flow.

	Reworded Data	Demanded Quality	Quality Characteristic	Function	Reliability	Comments
1.	Wallet feels smooth when I hold it. Wallet slides smoothly from pocket.		Smoothness			
2.	Wallet is easy to remove.	Removes from pocket easily. Removes from purse easily.				
3.	I have easy access to contents.	Contents are accessed easily.				
4.	I can carry money.	Carries money easily.				

Figure 10-2. Wallace Wallet Works VOCT, part 2

	Reworded Data	Demanded Quality	Quality Characteristic	Function	Reliability	Comments
5.	I can carry as many items as I want.	Carries many items easily.				
	I can carry a variety of credit cards.	Carries credit cards easily.				I want to avoid carrying too much cash.
6.	I want contents to be visible.	Contents can be seen easily.			Windows that don't cloud.	Clear plastic windows.
	I want fast access to contents.	Contents can be accessed easily.				
7.	I can carry many items.			Holds pictures. Holds letters.		
8.	I want it to last a long time.				Lasts a long time.	
	I like the one I have.				Retains shape.	

Figure 10-2. Wallace Wallet Works VOCT, part 2, continued

	Reworded Data	Demanded Quality	Quality Characteristic	Function	Reliability	Comments
9.	I want a low price.					Price is important.
10.	I want to calculate any checkbook balances.					Provide calculator.

Figure 10-2. Wallace Wallet Works VOCT, part 2, continued

Chart A-1

This chart is composed of two main components. The first component, A-1, part 1, contains sections one through nine and concentrates on demanded quality. The second component contains sections 10 through 15 and focuses on quality characteristics. Each component will be explained in detail. See figure 10-3.

Chart A-1, Part 1

Chart A-1, part 1 has nine sections as shown in figure 10-4. Usually section 1 is called the demanded quality table, and sections 2 through 9 are called the quality planning table. Each section is defined as follows.

Section 1: Demanded quality table
Place the hierarchy of demanded quality

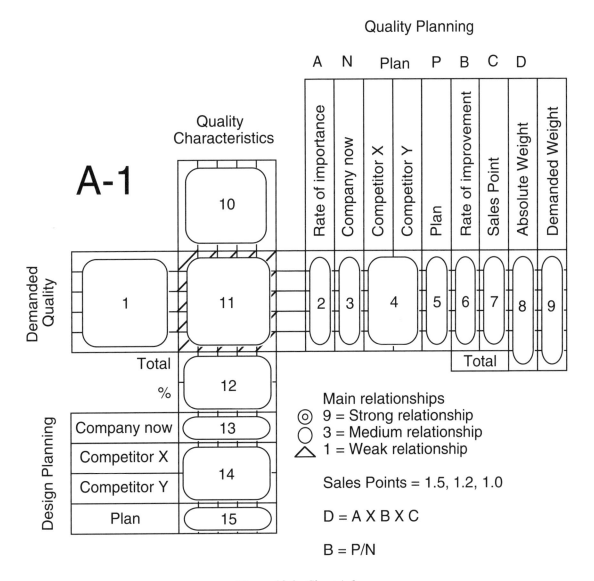

Figure 10-3. Chart A-1

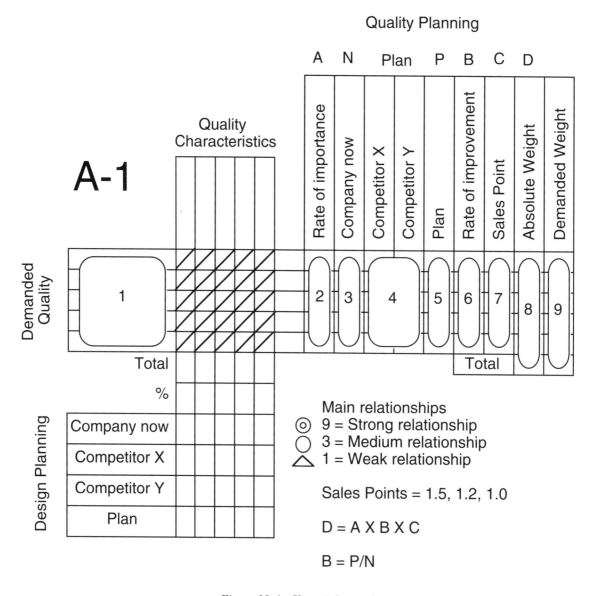

Figure 10-4. Chart A-1, part 1

items developed from the demanded quality column of the VOCT. The levels for demanded quality items are structured using the Affinity Diagram[1] and Tree Diagram.[2] In actual practice the team should try for three levels of detail in the Demanded Quality Tree Diagram. In the development of the diagram for the case study some demanded quality items from the VOCT appear as first level and others as second level, as shown in figure 10-5. For this illustration, we use only those items shown in the second level.

Section 2: Rating of importance
List the customer rating of importance for each demanded quality item using a scale of one through five, where one is low and five is high.

Section 3: Company now
Describe where the company is today regarding each demanded quality item. Usually, a scale of one to five is used in this section, but other scales may be used. It is most important to determine numbers based upon information from the customers.

Section 4: Competitor
Note that figure 10-4 has two competitors for this example. If we need to list three, or four, or more, this section would be modified as such. List how each competitor is doing in regard to each demanded quality item. Usually, a scale of one to five is used. As in section 3, it is most important to determine numbers based upon information from the customers.

Section 5: Plan
List the plan for each demanded quality item, using the same scale as section 2. This plan should be based on the analyses of sections 2, 3, and 4.

Section 6: Rate of improvement
Develop a result by dividing the value for each demanded quality item in section 5 by the value for each demanded quality item in section 3.

Section 7: Sales points
List the level of sales points for each demanded quality item with a 1.5 for a strong sales point, a 1.2 for a lesser sales point, and 1.0 for items that are not sales points.

Section 8: Absolute weight
Establish a weight for each demanded quality item by multiplying the values in section 2 by the values in section 6 by the number in section 7.

---

[1] This tool gathers large amounts of language data (ideas, opinions, issues, etc.) and organizes it into groups based on the natural relationship between each item. It is largely a creative rather than logical process. *The Memory Jogger Plus+*™, by Michael Brassard, GOAL/QPC, © 1989.

[2] This tool systematically maps out in increasing detail the full range of paths and tasks that need to be accomplished in order to achieve a primary goal and every related subgoal. Graphically, it resembles an organization chart or family tree. *The Memory Jogger Plus+*™, by Michael Brassard, GOAL/QPC, © 1989.

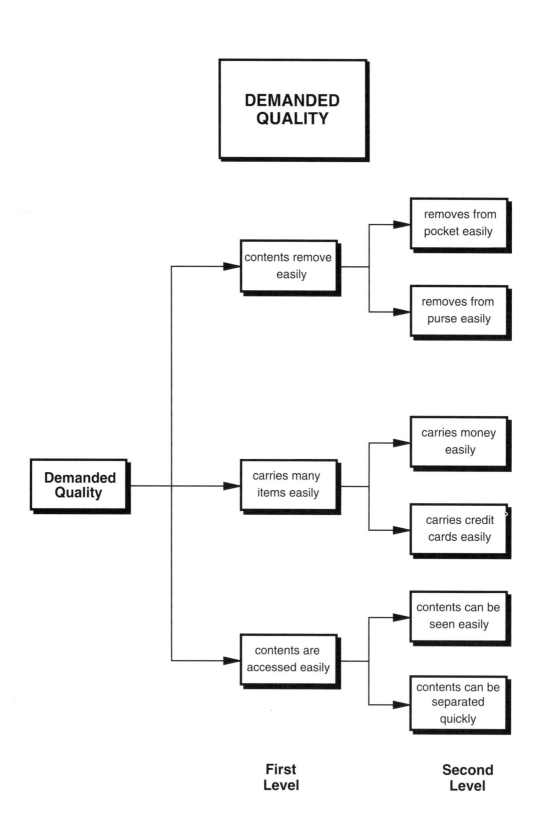

Figure 10-5. Wallace Wallet Works Demanded Quality Tree

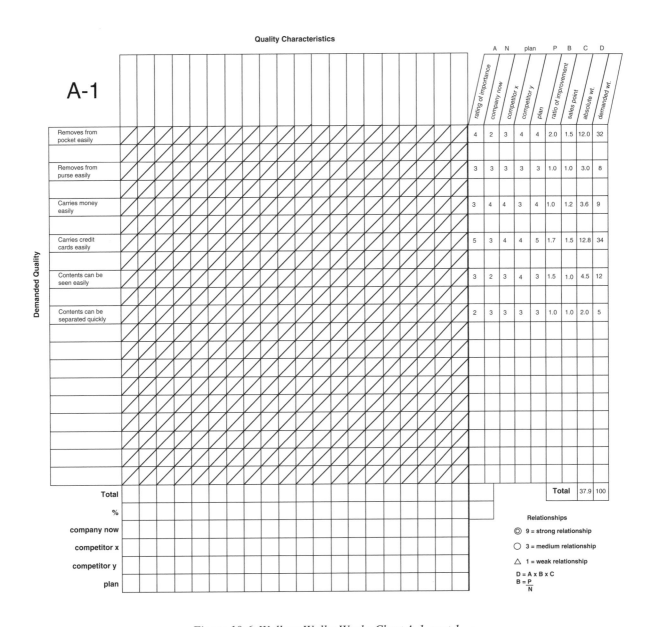

Figure 10-6. Wallace Wallet Works Chart A-1, part 1

Section 9: Demanded weight
This section establishes the demanded weight by converting the absolute weight to a percentage.

The Demanded Quality Tree for the Wallace Wallet Works is shown in figure 10-5. Chart A-1, part 1 for the Wallace Wallet Works case study is shown in figure 10-6.

Developing Quality Characteristics

Quality characteristics are measurable items that ensure the demanded quality requirement will be met. Each quality characteristic should:

1. Be a measurable item. The measurement will ensure we meet the demanded quality as defined by the voice of the customer.

2. Be devoid of words that refer to:
   - Functions
   - Means
   - Cost
   - Price
   - Reliability (including failure mode)
   - Demanded Quality
   - Elements
   - Tests
   - Process steps
   - Safety

The adapted use of a Cause and Effect Diagram in the vertical direction, as shown in figure 10-7, is a way to focus the team on developing quality characteristics from demanded quality items. The Cause and Effect Diagram is adapted to focus the QFD team on one demanded quality element at a time.

Figure 10-8 illustrates the vertical Cause and Effect Diagram approach to develop quality characteristics for the Wallace Wallet Works' customer demand "contents can be seen easily." This approach requires a separate vertical Cause and Effect Diagram for each demanded quality entry. The items developed on the branches of each vertical Cause and Effect Diagram can then be combined using an Affinity Diagram as shown in the steps for Chart A-1, part 2.

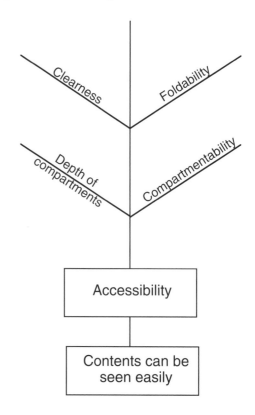

Figure 10-7. Cause and Effect Diagram

Figure 10-8. Wallace Wallet Works Cause and Effect Diagram

Once the Affinity Diagram is completed it can be further refined by using the Tree Diagram to obtain the appropriate level for each quality characteristic as shown in figure 10-9.

Another approach is to have the QFD team brainstorm a list of quality characteristics from scratch and then use the Affinity Diagram and Tree Diagram to arrange them by level. The facilitator or trainer must be careful with this approach to avoid overlooking demanded quality items.

Facilitators and trainers may find the vertical Cause and Effect Diagram an effective tool for keeping the QFD team focused during the development of the quality characteristics.

Chart A-1, Part 2

Chart A-1, part 2 has six sections as shown in figure 10-10. Section 10 is generally called the quality characteristics table. Sections 13 through 15 are called the design planning table. Each section is defined as follows:

Section 10: Quality characteristics table
Place first-level and second-level quality characteristics developed from the demanded quality column of the VOCT. In actual practice, the team should try for three levels of detail in the Quality Characteristics Tree Diagram. These levels are structured using the Affinity Diagram and Tree Diagram.

Section 11: Relationship matrix
Fill in the relationships between demanded quality items and quality characteristics using a double circle or 9 for strong, a single circle or 3 for medium, and a triangle or 1 for a weak relationship. Multiply each symbol by

the demanded weight for each demanded quality item and put the total in the box with the related symbol. This way of establishing importance is used in other charts for establishing weights for each item such as function, failure mode, concepts, and elements. At the completion of this step, the A-1 chart should be checked. This process is described in Chapter 11.

Section 12: Compute a weight for each quality characteristic
Calculate a total for each column of quality characteristics. If necessary, convert each weight for quality characteristics to a percentage.

Section 13: Company now
List the current value for each quality characteristic. In this case, use the following scale: 1 is best, 2 is satisfactory, and 3 is poor.

Section 14: Competitor
Although figure 10-10 has only two competitors for this section, it is possible to list as many as you have information on. These competitors should be the same as those listed in Chart A-1, part 1, section 4. The scale used to evaluate the competitors is 1 is best, 2 is satisfactory, and 3 is poor.

Section 15: Plan (target value)
This section lists a target value for each quality characteristic. Target values should be based on analysis of sections 12, 13, and 14.

Figure 10-11 shows the completed Chart A-1, part 2 for the Wallace Wallet Works case study. Figure 10-12 shows a completed Chart A-1 for the Wallace Wallet Works case study.

Quality Characteristics

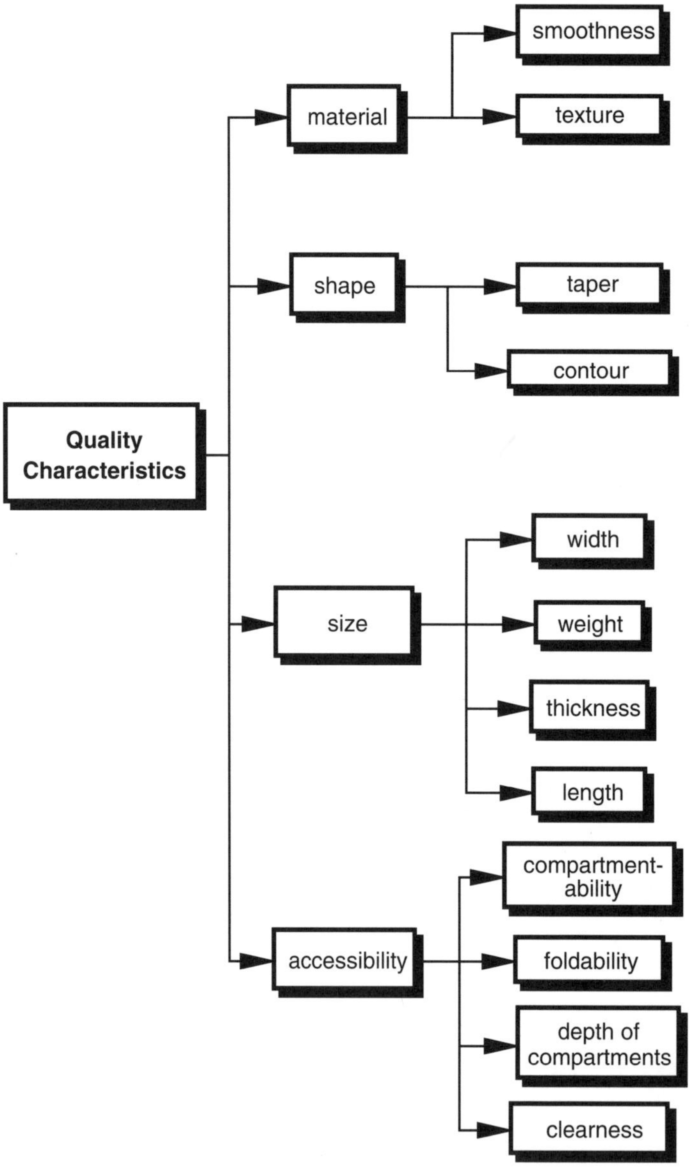

Figure 10-9. Wallace Wallet Works Tree Diagram

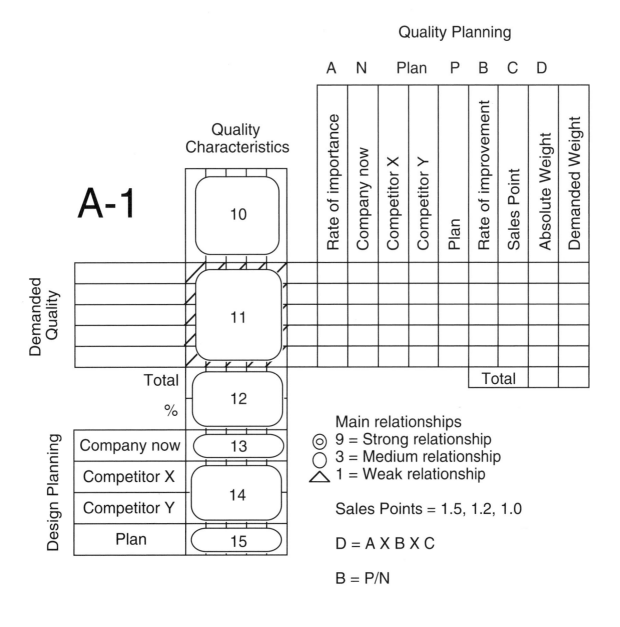

Figure 10-10. Chart A-1, part 2

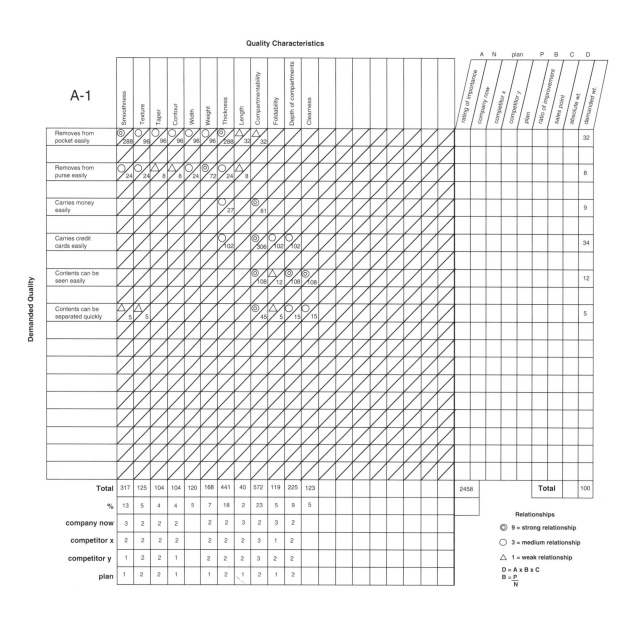

Figure 10-11. Wallace Wallet Works Chart A-1, part 2

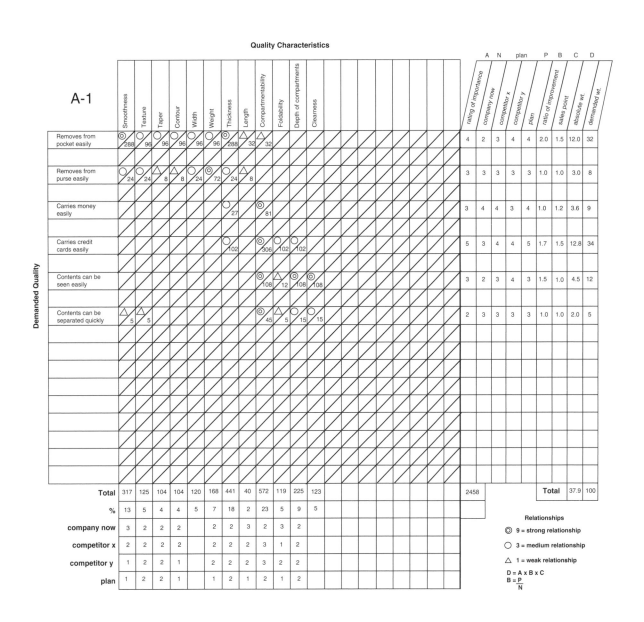

Figure 10-12. Wallace Wallet Works Chart A-1 (completed)

Building a Function Tree

Function Trees are developed by those people with product or service knowledge. Based on value analysis and value engineering methods, statements expressing function should have an active verb and an object (noun). A subject must also be included, so that we can clarify from where (such as the product or element or service) the particular function is coming. For this case study, we have chosen a wallet.

Brainstorm functions using the definition of functions, which are those tasks that are necessary for the product or service to be deliverable and acceptable to the customer. They constitute what the product or service does. The function(s) developed are used to build a Function Tree Diagram. We must add missing function(s) to the Function Tree from the Voice of the Customer Table (VOCT) as required for achieving demanded quality items. Function analysis is sufficient when a given Function Tree branch identifies concepts, which are methods for achieving functions. Figure 10-13 shows a Function Tree for the Wallace Wallet Works case study.

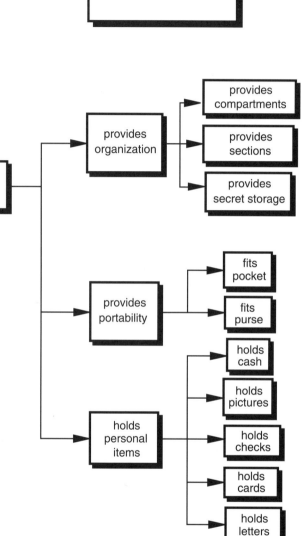

Figure 10-13. Wallace Wallet Works Function Tree

Building a Chart B-1

As shown in figure 10-14, Chart B-1 has seven sections. Each section is defined as follows:

Section 1: Functions
When structuring this section, place the functions from the Tree Diagram into this section.

Section 2: Demanded quality
Place the demanded quality items from Chart A-1 (Chart A-1, section 1).

Section 3: Demanded quality weight
Place the weight for demanded quality developed in Chart A-1, section 9.

Section 4: Relationships
Develop the relationships between demanded quality items and functions using a double circle for strong, a circle for medium, and a triangle for weak relationships. A weight for each box is calculated by multiplying the value of the relationship symbol by the demanded quality weight for that row.

Section 1': Addition of missing or new function(s)
If we add missing or new function(s) in section 1', it is necessary to do the entire section 4 again.

Section 5: Column totals
Total the values for each column of functions, and add these totals for a grand total.

Section 5': Function weight
Convert each weight for functions to a percentage, using the grand total.

Figure 10-15 shows a completed Chart B-1 for the Wallace Wallet Works case study.

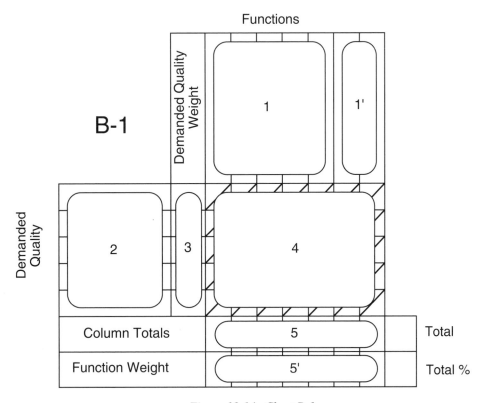

Figure 10-14. Chart B-1

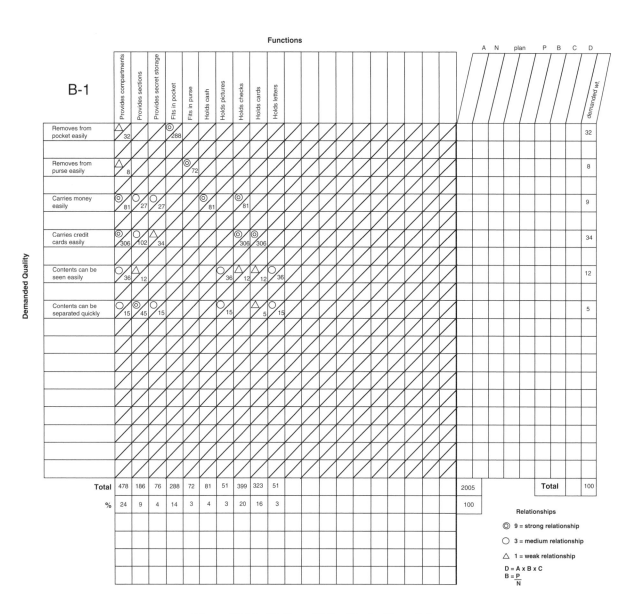

Figure 10-15. Wallace Wallet Works Chart B-1

Building Chart A-2

As shown in figure 10-16, Chart A-2 has six sections. Each section is defined as follows:

Section 1: Functions
Place all functions from Chart B-1.

Section 2: Quality characteristics
Place the quality characteristics from Chart A-1, section 10.

Section 3: Quality characteristic weight
Place the weights for quality characteristics as developed in Chart A-1, section 12 in this section.

Section 4: Relationships
Fill in the relationships between quality characteristics and functions using a double circle for strong, a circle for medium, and a triangle for a weak relationship. A weight for each box is calculated by multiplying the value of the relationship symbol by the quality characteristic weight for that row.

Section 5: Column weight
Total the values for each function column and sum these columns.

Section 5': Function weight
Convert each weight for functions to a percentage.

Figure 10-17 shows a completed Chart A-2 for the Wallace Wallet Works case study.

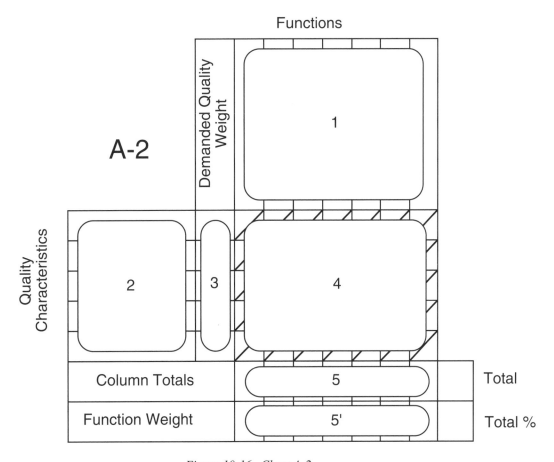

Figure 10-16. Chart A-2

Functions

A-2

Strong Relationship: ⊚ 9
Medium Relationship: ○ 3
Weak Relationship: △ 1

Quality Characteristics	Provides compartments	Provides sections	Provides secret storage	Fits in pocket	Fits in purse	Holds cash	Holds pictures	Holds checks	Holds cards	Holds letters		Quality Characteristic Weight
Smoothness	⊚ 117	△ 13		⊚ 117	○ 39	○ 39	△ 13		△ 13	△ 13		13
Texture	△ 5			○ 15	○ 15							5
Taper				○ 12	△ 4							4
Contour				△ 4	△ 4							4
Width	△ 5	△ 5							⊚ 45			5
Weight					△ 7	○ 21						7
Thickness	○ 54			○ 54	○ 18			⊚ 162				18
Length									○ 6			2
Compartmentability	⊚ 207	○ 69	○ 69	△ 23		△ 23		⊚ 207	○ 69			23
Foldability	△ 5	○ 15		△ 5								5
Depth of compartments			○ 27				△ 9		⊚ 81	△ 9		9
Clearness	○ 15						⊚ 45		⊚ 45	⊚ 45		5
Column Totals	408	102	96	230	87	83	67	369	259	67		Total 1768
Function Weight %	23	6	5	13	5	5	4	21	15	3		Total 100%

Figure 10-17. Wallace Wallet Works Chart A-2

Comparing function weights from Chart A-2 and Chart B-1

Upon completing the charts for function deployment, we will have function weights from Chart B-1 and Chart A-2. The top ranking functions (at least the top three) should be the same for Chart A-2 and Chart B-1, although the order may differ, because both sets of weights are based upon demanded quality. If we find different ranking, Charts A-1, B-1, and A-2 must be reviewed for the following:

- The demanded quality hierarchy in Chart A-1.
- The quality characteristics hierarchy in Chart A-1.
- Are there missing items for demanded quality, quality characteristics, or functions?

- The relationships are reasonable in each chart.
- The calculations for each item are correct.

In the Wallace Wallet Works case, the top functions for Chart B-1 and Chart A-2 agree so further analysis is not required.

Building Chart D-2

Chart D-2 is used to attain an early estimate of product failure modes that may negatively impact the development of required functions. The prioritized failure modes should be reviewed and resolved via reliability analysis.

As shown in figure 10-18, Chart D-2 has six sections. Each section is defined as follows:

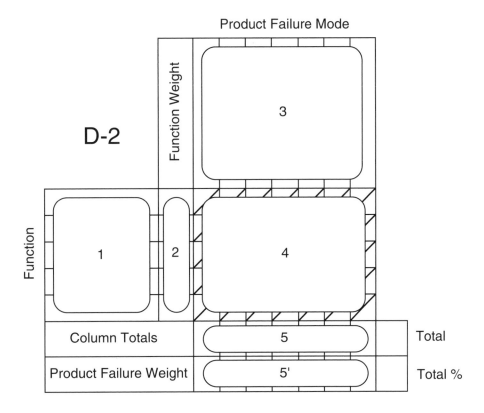

Figure 10-18. Chart D-2

Section 1: Functions
Carry over functions from Chart A-2.

Section 2: Function weight
The function weights are carried from Chart A-2, section 3.

Section 3: Product failure mode
Place the lowest levels from the Fault Tree in this section.

Section 4: Relationships
Fill in the relationships between functions and product failure modes using a double circle for a strong relationship, a circle for medium, and a triangle for a weak relationship. A weight for each box is calculated by multiplying the function weight by the value of the symbol.

Section 5: Column total
Total the numbers for each column for product/service failure modes and sum.

Section 5': Failure mode weight
Convert each weight for product/service failure modes to a percentage.

Figure 10-19 shows the product fault tree for the wallet.

Figure 10-20 shows the complete Chart D-2 for the Wallace Wallet Works.

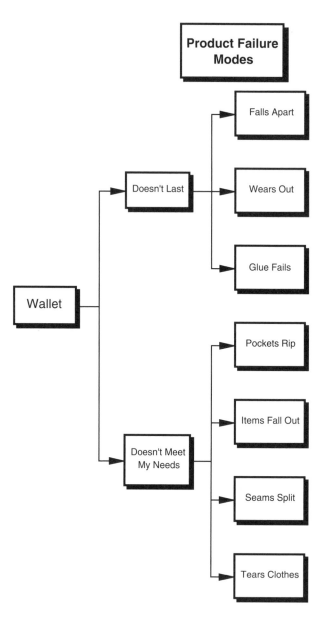

Figure 10-19. Wallace Wallet Works Product Fault Tree

Product Failure Modes

D-2

Strong Relationship: ◎ 9
Medium Relationship: ○ 3
Weak Relationship: △ 1

Functions

Function	Falls apart	Wears out	Items fall out	Seams split	Tears clothes	Glue fails	Pockets rip					Function Weight
Provides compartments	◎ 207	◎ 207	○ 69	○ 69		◎ 207	○ 69					23
Provides sections	◎ 54		○ 18	○ 18		○ 18	○ 18					6
Provides secret storage	◎ 108	△ 12	○ 36	△ 12								13
Fits in pocket				△ 6	◎ 54							6
Fits in purse				△ 5	◎ 45							5
Holds cash	◎ 45	○ 15										5
Holds pictures				△ 4	△ 4							4
Holds checks	◎ 189	○ 63										21
Holds cards	◎ 135	○ 45										15
Holds letters				△ 3	△ 3							3
Column Total	747	343	126	118	99	232	87					Total 1752
Product/Service failure mode %	43	20	7	7	5	13	5					Total 100%

Figure 10-20. Wallace Wallet Works Chart D-2

Building Chart C-3

As shown in figure 10-21, Chart C-3 has six sections. Each section is defined as follows:

Section 1: Concepts
Brainstorm concepts for accomplishing given functions based upon Chart A-2.

Section 2: Quality characteristics
Place the quality characteristics from Chart A-1.

Section 3: Quality characteristics weight
The quality characteristic weights are carried from Chart A-1, section 12.

Section 4: Relationships
Fill in the relationships between quality characteristics and concepts using a double circle for strong, a circle for medium, and a triangle for weak relationships. Calculate a value for each relationship by multiplying the characteristic weight by the symbol value.

Section 5: Column total
Total each concept column and sum the results.

Section 5': Concept weight
Convert the column total to a percentage.

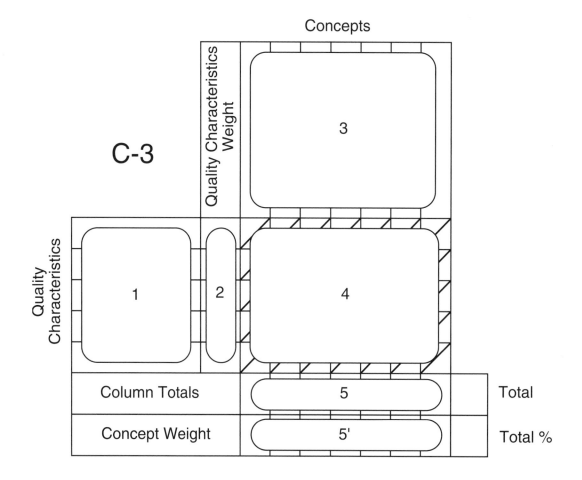

Figure 10-21. Chart C-3

Figure 10-22 shows the brainstorming list that the QFD team developed around new concepts that might be feasible replacements for some existing functions of the wallet. It also shows how the wallet is constructed now.

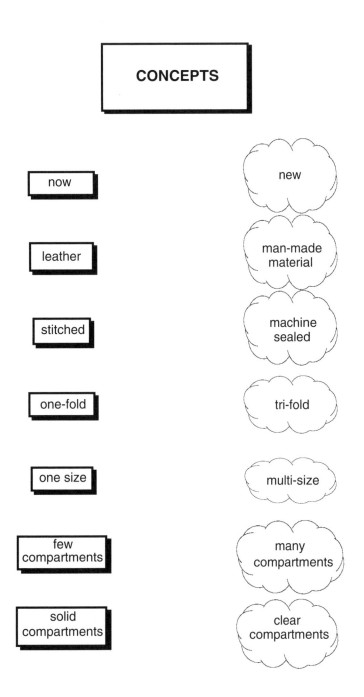

Figure 10-22. Wallace Wallet Works Brainstorming List

Concepts

C-3

Strong Relationship: ◎ 9
Medium Relationship: ○ 3
Weak Relationship: △ 1

Quality Characteristics	Leather	Man-made fabric	Stitched	Machine sealed	Onefold	Trifold	One size	Multi size	Few compartments	Many compartments	Solid compartments	Clear compartments	Quality Characteristic Weight
Smoothness		◎ 117		○ 39		△ 13		△ 13					13
Texture		○ 15						△ 5					5
Taper				△ 4		△ 4		△ 4		○ 12			4
Contour				△ 4		△ 4		△ 4		○ 12			4
Width										◎ 45		△ 5	5
Weight		○ 21		△ 7		△ 7		○ 21		◎ 63			7
Thickness		○ 54		○ 54		◎ 162		○ 54		○ 54			18
Length						○ 6		○ 6		◎ 18			2
Compartmentability		△ 23				○ 69		◎ 207		◎ 207		○ 69	23
Foldability		△ 5				◎ 45		△ 5		○ 15		○ 15	5
Depth of compartments		○ 27		△ 9				△ 9		◎ 81		△ 9	9
Clearness										△ 5		◎ 45	5
Column Totals		262		117		310		328		512		143	Total 1672
Concept Weight %		15		7		19		20		30		9	Total 100%

Figure 10-23 shows the Wallace Wallet Works Chart C-3, concept deployment.

Figure 10-23. Wallace Wallet Works Chart C-3

Building Chart E-3

As shown in figure 10-24, Chart E-3 has seven sections. Each section is defined as follows:

Section 1: Key concepts
When structuring this section, we should select and place the top-ranked concepts described in Chart C-3.

Section 2: Current method
List the current methods for satisfying functions.

Section 3: Quality characteristics
Place the quality characteristics from Chart A-1 (figure 10-11, section 10). For this case study, all the quality characteristics will be carried over from Chart A-1.

Section 4: Target value
Target values for each quality characteristic are carried over from Chart A-1, section 12.

Section 5: Relationships
This section uses the symbols plus (+), minus (-), and same (S). Compare the top-ranked concepts with the current method and make the following decisions:

- If the concept would better accomplish a target value for each quality characteristic than the current method, put a plus (+) in each box.

- If the concept would accomplish a target value for each quality characteristic less effectively than the current method, put a minus (-) in each box.

- If the concept and current methods are equally effective at accomplishing a target value for each quality characteristic, put an "S" in each box.

Section 6: +'s
Total the pluses (+) for each concept column.

Section 7: -'s
Total the minuses (-) for each concept column.

Selecting key concepts
When selecting concepts for capability deployment, we should not combine pluses (+) and minuses (-) in Chart E-3; instead we should select concepts that have the most pluses (+).

Review and analyze any minuses. Try to convert them to pluses.

Figure 10-25 shows the Wallace Wallet Works Chart E-3, concept analysis.

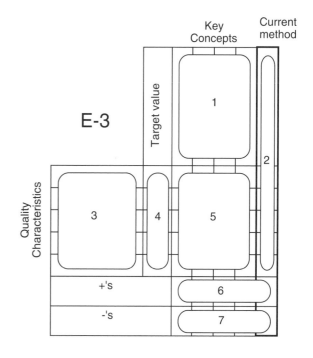

Figure 10-24. Chart E-3

Key Concepts

E-3

Quality Characteristics	One-fold	Tri-fold	One size	Multi-size	Few compartments	Many compartments		Quality Characteristic Target Value
Smoothness		S		S		S		1
Texture		S		S		S		2
Taper		S		S		S		2
Contour		S		S		S		1
Width		+		+		-		1
Weight		S		+		-		2
Thickness		S		+		S		1
Length		+		+		-		2
Compartmentability		+		S		+		1
Foldability		+		S		+		2
Depth of compartments		S		S		+		2
Clearness		S		S		S		1
+'s		4+		4+		3+		
-'s						3-		

Figure 10-25. Wallace Wallet Works Chart E-3

Building Chart A-3'

As shown in figure 10-26, Chart A-3' has two sections. This chart is useful for the early identification of development areas that may potentially conflict with one another.

Section 1:
Carry over the functions from Chart A-2, and place them on both the horizontal and vertical axes.

Section 2:
Address each function individually and determine its potential interaction with all other functions. Place a check mark (✔) in those boxes where interaction may occur. Since these interactions are mirror images of each other, we only fill them in on one side of the matrix. Areas showing relationships should be analyzed for positive or negative effects. Negative effects are potential bottle-necks to project success.

Figure 10-27 is a filled-in example of the Wallace Wallet Works case study. An example of interaction is between "fits in pocket" versus "holds letters." This was determined to be a negative interaction.

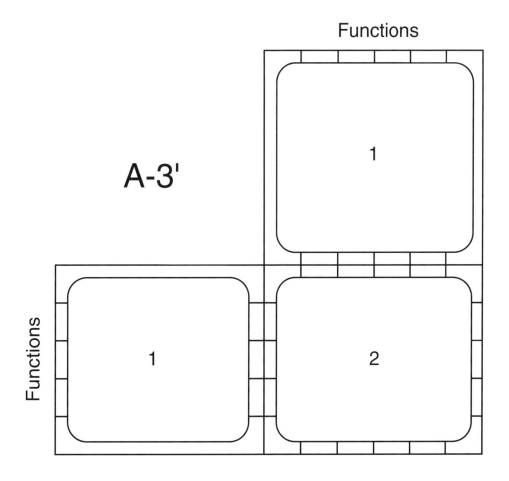

Figure 10-26. Chart A-3'

Functions

A-3'	Provides compartments	Provides sections	Holds cards	Holds checks	Holds cash	Fits in pocket	Fits in purse	Provides secret section	Holds pictures	Holds letters
Provides compartments						✓	✓			
Provides sections						✓	✓			
Holds cards				✓	✓				✓	✓
Holds checks									✓	✓
Holds cash									✓	✓
Fits in pocket							✓		✓	✓
Fits in purse										
Provides secret section										
Holds pictures										✓
Holds letters										

Figure 10-27. Wallace Wallet Works Chart A-3'

Building Chart A-4

Chart A-4 establishes a weight for each element based upon the quality characteristics. Element deployment identifies the relationships between elements and quality characteristics. An element is an item needed to allow the proposed concepts to perform. As shown in figure 10-28, Chart A-4 has five sections. Each section is defined as follows:

Section 1: Elements
The necessary elements are based on selected concepts and are developed using the Affinity Diagram and the Tree process.

Section 2: Quality characteristics
Place quality characteristics from Chart A-1. These are the same quality characteristics as those in Charts E-3 and A-4.

Section 3: Quality characteristic weight
This section uses the same quality characteristic weights as those in Chart C-3.

Section 4: Relationships
Fill in the relationships between quality characteristics and functions using a double circle for strong, a circle for medium, and a triangle for weak relationships. A weight for each box is calculated by multiplying the quality characteristic value by the relationship symbol value.

Section 5: Column total
Total each element column and sum.

Section 5': Element weight
Convert each weight for elements to a percentage.

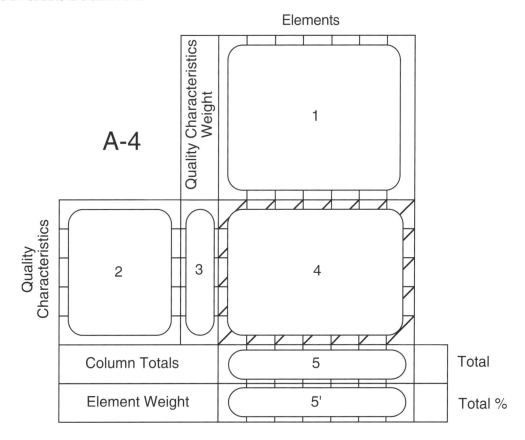

Figure 10-28. Chart A-4

Figure 10-29 shows a completed element list
for the Wallace Wallet Works. This is a
brainstormed list.

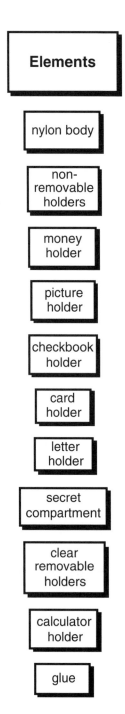

Figure 10-29. Wallace Wallet Works Element List

Figure 10-30 shows a completed Chart A-4 for the Wallace Wallet Works case study.

Elements

A-4

Strong Relationship: ◎ 9
Medium Relationship: ○ 3
Weak Relationship: △ 1

Quality Characteristics	Nylon body	Non-removable holder	Money holder	Picture holder	Checkbook holder	Card holder	Letter holder	Secret compartment	Clear removable holder	Calculator holder	Glue	Quality Characteristic Weight
Smoothness	◎ 117	△ 13						△ 13				13
Texture	○ 15	△ 5									△ 5	5
Taper												4
Contour		△ 4								△ 4		4
Width		○ 15	△ 5	○ 15	○ 15	○ 15	○ 15	△ 5	△ 5	○ 15		5
Weight	○ 21	○ 21	○ 21	○ 21	○ 21	○ 21	○ 21	△ 7	△ 7	△ 7		7
Thickness	○ 54	○ 54	△ 18	△ 18	△ 18	△ 18	△ 18	○ 54				18
Length	○ 6	◎ 18		△ 2	△ 2	△ 2	△ 2			○ 6		2
Compartmentability	◎ 207	○ 69	○ 69	○ 69	○ 69	○ 69	○ 69	◎ 207	○ 69		◎ 207	23
Foldability	△ 5		△ 5	◎ 45		○ 15	△ 5	△ 5	○ 15			5
Depth of compartments		○ 27	◎ 81	◎ 81	△ 9	◎ 81	◎ 81	◎ 81	○ 27	△ 9		9
Clearness		△ 5		○ 15					◎ 45			5
Column Totals	191	357	212	224	179	206	221	237	296	106	238	Total 2467
Element Weight %	8	14	9	9	7	8	9	10	12	4	10	Total 100%

Figure 10-30. Wallace Wallet Works Chart A-4

Building Chart D-4

Chart D-4 is called reliability deployment. It is usually the final step in the QFD design process. Its purpose is to flag key failure modes and to resolve them before continuing in the design and development process.

As shown in figure 10-31, Chart D-4 has six sections. Each section is defined as follows:

Section 1: Element failure modes
Determine element failure modes via a fault tree. Place lowest level failure modes in this section.

Section 2: Elements
When structuring this section, carry over the elements from Chart A-4.

Section 3: Element weight
The elements' weights are carried over from Chart A-4.

Section 4: Relationships
In this section, fill in the relationships between key elements and element failure modes using the double circle for strong, a circle for medium, and a triangle for a weak relationship. A weight for each box is calculated by multiplying the element weight by the value of the symbol.

Section 5: Column total
Total each column for element failure mode and sum.

Section 5': Element failure mode weight
Convert each weight for product/service failure modes to a percentage.

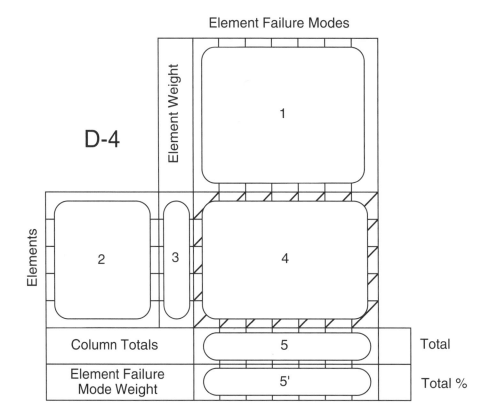

Figure 10-31. Chart D-4

Figure 10-32 shows the Element Fault Tree
for the wallet.

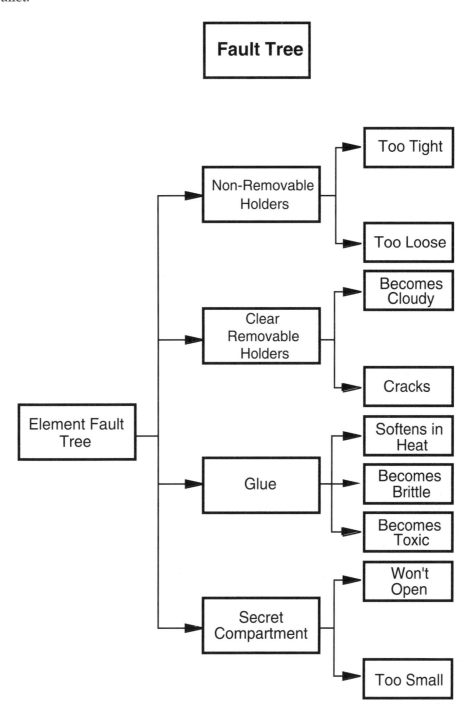

Figure 10-32. Wallace Wallet Works Element Fault Tree

Figure 10-33 shows the completed Chart D-4 for the Wallace Wallet Works.

Element Failure Mode

D-4

Strong Relationship: ◎ 9
Medium Relationship: ○ 3
Weak Relationship: △ 1

Elements	Too tight	Too loose	Becomes cloudy	Cracks	Softens in heat	Becomes brittle	Becomes toxic	Won't open	Too small			Element Weight
Nylon body	◎ 72			○ 24	○ 24		△ 8	△ 8				8
Non-removable holder	○ 42	○ 42		○ 42					◎ 126			14
Money holder	○ 27	○ 27							◎ 81			9
Picture holder	◎ 81	○ 27							○ 27			9
Checkbook holder		○ 21		○ 21					◎ 63			7
Card holder	○ 24	○ 24	△ 8						◎ 72			8
Letter holder	○ 27	○ 27							◎ 81			9
Secret compartment	◎ 90	○ 10						◎ 90	◎ 90			10
Clear removable holder			◎ 108	○ 36	○ 36	○ 36	○ 36		○ 36			12
Calculator holder		○ 12				△ 4			○ 12			4
Glue												10
Column Totals	363	190	116	123	60	40	44	98	588			Total 1622
Element failure mode weight %	22	12	7	8	4	2	3	6	36			Total 100%

Figure 10-33. Wallace Wallet Works Chart D-4

You have just been guided through a rather comprehensive QFD example. To review, we identified the elements required to allow the concepts to perform their associated functions, which are based upon demanded quality as described in the voice of the customer. We identified the measurable characteristics that must be in place to ensure we meet the demanded quality. We also identified potential failure modes to avoid discovering these failures after the process is operating.

Chapter 11

Reviewing Chart A-1

After a QFD team completes the relationships in Chart A-1, the facilitator should lead the team through a review of the chart to ensure it is complete and that all possibilities have been considered. This chapter details nine potential problem areas a facilitator should be aware of when conducting a Chart A-1 relationship review. These potential problem areas should also be covered during training ses-sions to make participants aware of them and of the importance of detecting them at this stage.

Reasons for Reviewing Chart A-1

It is necessary to determine that the relationships are as accurate as possible and to gain confidence in the validity of the decision-making process used to produce Chart A-1. This review is necessary because a weight for each quality characteristic will be established based on the relationships in Chart A-1, and weights for each quality characteristic will also be used in the other charts after Chart A-1. There is no such thing as a perfect Chart A-1 because QFD handles language data, not number data. However, it is important to review to see if any of the following problems are apparent. (All problems illustrated are for Chart A-1 only.)

Chart A-1

Demanded Quality	QC 1.1.1	QC 1.1.2	QC 1.1.3	QC 1.2.1	QC 1.2.2	QC 2.1.1	QC 2.1.2	QC 2.1.3	QC 2.1.4	QC 2.2.1	QC 2.2.2	QC 3.1.1	QC 3.1.2	QC 3.2.1	QC 3.2.2	QC 3.2.3
DQ 1.1.1	◎		○		△	△										
DQ 1.1.2 ←																
DQ 1.2.1		◎			◎	△				○	◎					○
DQ 1.2.2				○		◎							△			
DQ 1.2.3			△				○		◎		△	○			◎	
DQ 2.1.1 ←																
DQ 2.1.2			◎	○			○				○			◎		
DQ 2.2.1		◎			△							◎				○
DQ 2.2.2						◎		○					△			◎
DQ 2.2.3	◎				◎					○					△	
DQ 2.2.4					◎		○		○	◎		○				

Figure 11-1. Problem 1

Problem 1 (figure 11-1)

This example shows some demanded quality (DQ) items that have no relationships with quality characteristics. If DQ 1.1.2 or DQ 2.1.1 of figure 11-1 are demanded quality items, we cannot measure or control them. Each quality characteristic should be based on demanded quality items. If there is not at least one quality characteristic to meet a given demanded quality item, then we should develop a new quality characteristic.

Chart A-1	Quality Characteristic / Demanded Quality		QC 1					QC 2						QC 3				
			QC 1.1			QC 1.2		QC 2.1				QC 2.2		QC 3.1		QC 3.2		
			QC 1.1.1	QC 1.1.2	QC 1.1.3	QC 1.2.1	QC 1.2.2	QC 2.1.1	QC 2.1.2	QC 2.1.3	QC 2.1.4	QC 2.2.1	QC 2.2.2	QC 3.1.1	QC 3.1.2	QC 3.2.1	QC 3.2.2	QC 3.2.3
DQ 1	DQ 1.1	DQ 1.1.1	◎		○		△	△										
		DQ 1.1.2				◎					○					○		
	DQ 1.2	DQ 1.2.1			◎		◎		△			○	◎					○
		DQ 1.2.2				○		◎										
		DQ 1.2.3		△					○		◎		△	◎			◎	
DQ 2	DQ 2.1	DQ 2.1.1					△					◎				△		
		DQ 2.1.2			◎	○			○				○			◎		
	DQ 2.2	DQ 2.2.1		◎			△							◎				○
		DQ 2.2.2						◎										◎
		DQ 2.2.3	◎			◎						○					△	
		DQ 2.2.4					◎		○		○	◎		○				

Figure 11-2. Problem 2

Problem 2 (figure 11-2)
This example shows some quality characteristics that have no relationships with demanded quality items. In this case, Chart A-1 might be too large, containing an unnecessary quality characteristic(s). We do not need to place this quality characteristic(s) at the top of the chart. We should identify where the quality characteristics come from, since some quality characteristics are not based on demanded quality items.

Chart A-1 — Quality Characteristic vs. Demanded Quality

Demanded Quality	QC 1.1.1	QC 1.1.2	QC 1.1.3	QC 1.2.1	QC 1.2.2	QC 2.1.1	QC 2.1.2	QC 2.1.3	QC 2.1.4	QC 2.2.1	QC 2.2.2	QC 3.1.1	QC 3.1.2	QC 3.2.1	QC 3.2.2	QC 3.2.3
DQ 1.1.1 ←			○		△	△										
DQ 1.1.2 ←								○						○		
DQ 1.2.1				◎	◎	△				○	◎					○
DQ 1.2.2					○	◎						○				
DQ 1.2.3			△				○		◎		△	◎			◎	
DQ 2.1.1					△		○		◎					△		
DQ 2.1.2 ←					○		○				○					
DQ 2.2.1		◎			△		△					◎				○
DQ 2.2.2						◎										◎
DQ 2.2.3	◎				◎					○			◎		△	
DQ 2.2.4					◎		○		○	◎		○				

Figure 11-3. Problem 3

Problem 3 (figure 11-3)

This example shows one or more demanded quality items that have no strong relationship with quality characteristics. This may indicate that there are no identified important quality characteristics. New quality characteristics will have to be developed.

Chart A-1 / Demanded Quality		Quality Characteristic	QC 1					QC 2						QC 3				
			QC 1.1			QC 1.2		QC 2.1				QC 2.2		QC 3.1		QC 3.2		
			QC 1.1.1	QC 1.1.2	QC 1.1.3	QC 1.2.1	QC 1.2.2	QC 2.1.1	QC 2.1.2	QC 2.1.3	QC 2.1.4	QC 2.2.1	QC 2.2.2	QC 3.1.1	QC 3.1.2	QC 3.2.1	QC 3.2.2	QC 3.2.3
DQ 1	DQ 1.1	DQ 1.1.1	◎		○		△	△										
		DQ 1.1.2	◎		○		△	△										
	DQ 1.2	DQ 1.2.1			◎		◎	△				○	◎					○
		DQ 1.2.2				○		◎							○			
		DQ 1.2.3		△						○	◎	△	◎				◎	
DQ 2	DQ 2.1	DQ 2.1.1					△		○			◎				△		
		DQ 2.1.2	◎		○		△	△										
	DQ 2.2	DQ 2.2.1		◎			△			△				◎				○
		DQ 2.2.2					◎											◎
		DQ 2.2.3	◎			◎									◎	△		
		DQ 2.2.4					◎	○			○	◎		○				

Figure 11-4. Problem 4

Problem 4 (figure 11-4)

This example shows some demanded quality items that have identical relationships with every given quality characteristic. In this case, the key quality characteristics are probably misunderstood. This happens because an incorrect hierarchy of demanded quality items has been constructed. The hierarchy of demanded quality items should be reviewed for completeness.

Figure 11-5. Problem 5

Chart A-1 / Demanded Quality			QC 1					QC 2						QC 3				
			QC 1.1			QC 1.2		QC 2.1				QC 2.2		QC 3.1		QC 3.2		
			QC 1.1.1	QC 1.1.2	QC 1.1.3	QC 1.2.1	QC 1.2.2	QC 2.1.1	QC 2.1.2	QC 2.1.3	QC 2.1.4	QC 2.2.1	QC 2.2.2	QC 3.1.1	QC 3.1.2	QC 3.2.1	QC 3.2.2	QC 3.2.3
DQ 1	DQ 1.1	DQ 1.1.1	◎	◎	○													
		DQ 1.1.2	◎	○	○													
	DQ 1.2	DQ 1.2.1	△	◎	◎													
		DQ 1.2.2	△	◎	○													
		DQ 1.2.3							○		◎		△	◎			◎	
DQ 2	DQ 2.1	DQ 2.1.1				△			○		◎					△		
		DQ 2.1.2				△	△											
	DQ 2.2	DQ 2.2.1				△				△				◎				○
		DQ 2.2.2						◎										◎
		DQ 2.2.3				◎						○			◎	△		
		DQ 2.2.4					◎	○			○	◎		○				

Problem 5 (figure 11-5)

This example shows the relationships forming a block in some section of the chart. The key quality characteristics are probably misunderstood in this case. The hierarchy of demanded quality and quality characteristics should be reviewed.

Chart A-1 — Demanded Quality \ Quality Characteristic	QC 1.1.1	QC 1.1.2	QC 1.1.3	QC 1.2.1	QC 1.2.2	QC 2.1.1	QC 2.1.2	QC 2.1.3	QC 2.1.4	QC 2.2.1	QC 2.2.2	QC 3.1.1	QC 3.1.2	QC 3.2.1	QC 3.2.2	QC 3.2.3
DQ 1.1.1	◎		○		△	△		◎								
DQ 1.1.2				◎				○					○			
DQ 1.2.1			○		◎		△			○	◎					○
DQ 1.2.2				○		◎							△			
DQ 1.2.3	△	△	○	◎	○	◎		○	○	◎	△	◎	△	△	◎	◎
DQ 2.1.1				△							◎			△		
DQ 2.1.2			◎	○			○				○			◎		
DQ 2.2.1		◎			△							◎	○			○
DQ 2.2.2						◎		○								◎
DQ 2.2.3	◎			◎						○				△		
DQ 2.2.4					◎		○		○	◎		○				

Figure 11-6. Problem 6

Problem 6 (figure 11-6)

This example shows one of the demanded quality items that has a relationship with each or many of the quality characteristics. This case has two possible causes. One is that the demanded quality item(s) includes such other categories as cost, reliability, and safety. The other is that the first or second level demanded quality item(s) is placed on the third level in the demanded quality table. The rules for demanded quality items and the hierarchy of demanded quality items should be reviewed.

Chart A-1 — Demanded Quality vs. Quality Characteristic

Demanded Quality			QC 1.1			QC 1.2		QC 2.1				QC 2.2		QC 3.1		QC 3.2		
			QC 1.1.1	QC 1.1.2	QC 1.1.3	QC 1.2.1	QC 1.2.2	QC 2.1.1	QC 2.1.2	QC 2.1.3	QC 2.1.4	QC 2.2.1	QC 2.2.2	QC 3.1.1	QC 3.1.2	QC 3.2.1	QC 3.2.2	QC 3.2.3
DQ 1	DQ 1.1	DQ 1.1.1	◎		○		△	△		◎								
		DQ 1.1.2				◎		△			○					○		
	DQ 1.2	DQ 1.2.1			◎		◎	○	△			○	◎					○
		DQ 1.2.2				○		◎							△			
		DQ 1.2.3				○		◎		○			△	◎		△	◎	
DQ 2	DQ 2.1	DQ 2.1.1					△	◎				◎				△		
		DQ 2.1.2			◎	○		◎	○				○			◎		
	DQ 2.2	DQ 2.2.1		◎			△	△						◎	○			○
		DQ 2.2.2						◎	○									◎
		DQ 2.2.3	◎			◎		○				○					△	
		DQ 2.2.4					◎	○	○			○	◎	○				

Figure 11-7. Problem 7

Problem 7 (figure 11-7)

This example shows one of the quality characteristics that has relationships with each or many demanded quality items. This case has two possible causes. One is that the quality characteristic(s) includes such categories as cost, reliability, and safety. The other is that the first or second level quality characteristic(s) is placed on the third level in the quality characteristic table. The rules for quality characteristics and the hierarchy of quality characteristics should be reviewed.

Chart A-1 / Demanded Quality \ Quality Characteristic	QC 1					QC 2						QC 3				
	QC 1.1			QC 1.2		QC 2.1				QC 2.2		QC 3.1		QC 3.2		
	QC 1.1.1	QC 1.1.2	QC 1.1.3	QC 1.2.1	QC 1.2.2	QC 2.1.1	QC 2.1.2	QC 2.1.3	QC 2.1.4	QC 2.2.1	QC 2.2.2	QC 3.1.1	QC 3.1.2	QC 3.2.1	QC 3.2.2	QC 3.2.3
DQ 1 / DQ 1.1 / DQ 1.1.1	◎															
DQ 1.1.2		◎														
DQ 1.2 / DQ 1.2.1			◎	○												
DQ 1.2.2				◎	◎											
DQ 1.2.3						○	◎									
DQ 2 / DQ 2.1 / DQ 2.1.1									◎							
DQ 2.1.2									◎							
DQ 2.2 / DQ 2.2.1									◎	○						
DQ 2.2.2											◎	○				
DQ 2.2.3													◎	○		
DQ 2.2.4															◎	◎

Figure 11-8. Problem 8

Problem 8 (figure 11-8)

This example shows relationships forming a nearly diagonal line with no other relationships indicated. In this case, the demanded quality items include quality characteristics such as methodologies of design, but demanded quality items should only represent the voice of the customer. This case needs to be reviewed with more emphasis placed upon obtaining the voice of the customer.

Chart A-1 — Demanded Quality vs. Quality Characteristic matrix

Demanded Quality	QC 1.1.1	QC 1.1.2	QC 1.1.3	QC 1.2.1	QC 1.2.2	QC 2.1.1	QC 2.1.2	QC 2.1.3	QC 2.1.4	QC 2.2.1	QC 2.2.2	QC 3.1.1	QC 3.1.2	QC 3.2.1	QC 3.2.2	QC 3.2.3
DQ 1.1.1	◎		○		△	△		△			△				△	
DQ 1.1.2				◎						○		△	△	○		
DQ 1.2.1		△					△			○	◎			△	○	
DQ 1.2.2				○		◎		△						△		△
DQ 1.2.3		△		△		○					△	◎		△		
DQ 2.1.1		△		△	△	△				◎				△	△	
DQ 2.1.2		△		○		○		△		○				◎	△	
DQ 2.2.1		△		△		△				△		◎				○
DQ 2.2.2		△		△		◎										◎
DQ 2.2.3	◎	△								○					△	
DQ 2.2.4	△	△	△			○				○	◎	○				

Figure 11-9. Problem 9

Problem 9 (figure 11-9)

This example shows many weak relationships. If we can get a weight for each quality characteristic, it is a "fuzzy" weight. A clear quality characteristic(s) or a weight for each quality characteristic having only strong relationships should be determined.

This review process is very important because it highlights potential problem areas that can lead to incorrect conclusions later in the process.

Chapter 12

Using Software

As we have discussed throughout this text, QFD is a powerful tool for communicating among and between individuals and cross-functional team members. This communication process is often difficult and cumbersome as it involves numerous mathematical calculations, recording of what has been discussed by the team, and compilation of the voice of the customer information.

QFD software is the tool of choice to simplify these recording and mathematical processes. Currently there are three packages of software on the market designed specifically to perform QFD. Additionally, some teams use highly modified spreadsheets in an attempt to mimic QFD software, and several commercially available spreadsheet templates are available. This chapter describes how the ideal QFD system as we see it would perform if it were available.

Because QFD must be a flexible process designed to meet the team's requirements, the first criterion to judge any sofware package by is its ability to adapt to the team's needs. The team members must be able to use their QFD methodology without changing their basic inputs, calculations, or outputs. The software should be adaptable to support all the types of matrices the team is going to use, including tables as shown in figure 12-1.

I.D.	Customer Characteristics (who)		Voice of the Customer	Use										
				what		when		where		why		how		
	I/E	Data		I/E	Data	I/E	Data	I/E	Data	I/E	Data	I/E	Data

Figure 12-1. Voice of the Customer Table, Part 1

The QFD software used should mathematically support all calculations required by the team to produce the results desired. Because different teams might want to compare data through slightly different methods, the software's mathematical functions must be powerful, flexible, and easy to use. In addition, the results of these mathematical operations should be able to be displayed as a number of different types of charts to give a good visual representation of the data and to allow for quick visual analysis. As shown in figure 12-2, the types of charts available should include line, symbol, bar, pareto, pie, and line/symbol. Defining different mathematical formulas and changing chart types should be a simple process and should not require modification of data.

Another criterion for judging software is the ability to make notes and enter text in any given point in the QFD chart. You should be able to enter this data on any line of text or at any intersecting point, and entered data should not be dependent on any other information or correlation. There should be a way to highlight those cells that have note data.

The software should be able to sort information by different criteria such as by tree level, by weight of entered value, or alphabetically. This ability to sort allows the team to comparatively evaluate the information both within one matrix and between different matrices. Some of these different types of sorts are shown in figures 12-3, 12-4, and 12-5.

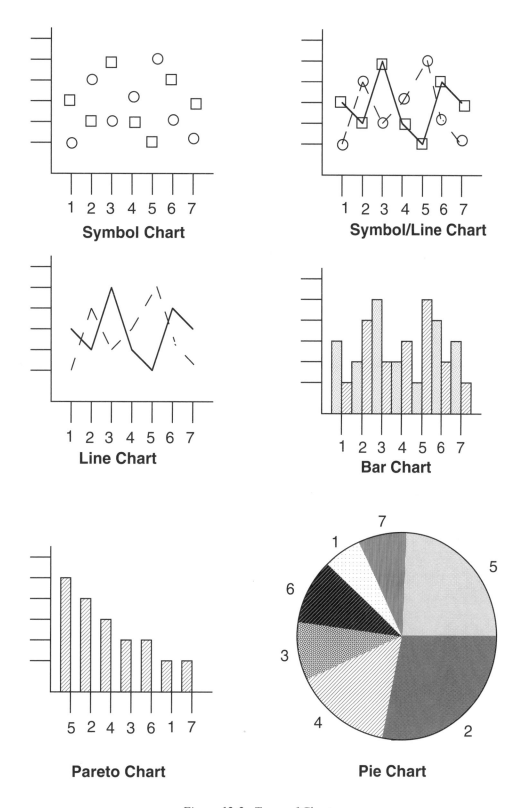

Figure 12-2. Types of Charts

Functions

A-2

Strong Relationship: ◎ 9
Medium Relationship: ○ 3
Weak Relationship: △ 1

Quality Characteristics

Characteristic	Provides compartments	Provides sections	Provides secret storage	Fits in pocket	Fits in purse	Holds cash	Holds pictures	Holds checks	Holds cards	Holds letters	Quality Characteristic Weight
Material — Smoothness	◎ 117	△ 13	◎ 117		○ 39	○ 39	△ 13		△ 13	△ 13	13
Material — Texture	△ 5			○ 15	○ 15						5
Shape — Taper				○ 12	△ 4						4
Shape — Contour				△ 4	△ 4						4
Size — Width	△ 5	△ 5							◎ 45		5
Size — Weight					△ 7	○ 21					7
Size — Thickness	○ 54			○ 54	△ 18			◎ 162			18
Size — Length									○ 6		2
Accessibility — Compartmentability	◎ 207	○ 69	○ 69	△ 23		△ 23		◎ 207	○ 69		23
Accessibility — Foldability	△ 5	○ 15		△ 5							5
Accessibility — Depth of compartments			○ 27				△ 9		◎ 81	△ 9	9
Accessibility — Clearness	○ 15						◎ 45		◎ 45	◎ 45	5
Column Totals	408	102	213	113	87	83	67	369	259	67	Total 1768
Function Weight %	23	6	13	6	5	5	4	21	15	3	Total 100%

Function groups: Provides organization (Provides compartments, Provides sections); Provides portability (Provides secret storage, Fits in pocket, Fits in purse); Holds personal items (Holds cash, Holds pictures, Holds checks, Holds cards, Holds letters).

Figure 12-3. Wallace Wallet Works Chart A-2, Sorted by Tree Level

Functions

A-2

Strong Relationship: ◎ 9

Medium Relationship: ○ 3

Weak Relationship: △ 1

Quality Characteristics	Provides compartments	Holds checks	Holds cards	Provides secret storage	Fits in pocket	Provides sections	Fits in purse	Holds cash	Holds pictures	Holds letters			Quality Characteristic Weight
Smoothness	◎ 117		△ 13	◎ 117	△ 13	○ 39	○ 39	△ 13	△ 13				13
Texture	△ 5				○ 15		○ 15						5
Taper					12		4						4
Contour					△ 4		△ 4						4
Width	△ 5		◎ 45			△ 5							5
Weight							○ 7	△ 21					7
Thickness	○ 54	◎ 162			○ 54		△ 18						18
Length			6										2
Compartmentability	◎ 207	◎ 207	○ 69	○ 69	△ 23	○ 69		△ 23					23
Foldability	△ 5				△ 5	○ 15							5
Depth of compartments			◎ 81	○ 27					△ 9	△ 9			9
Clearness	○ 15		◎ 45						◎ 45	◎ 45			5
Column Totals	408	369	259	213	113	102	87	83	67	67			Total 1768
Function Weight %	23	21	15	13	6	6	5	5	4	3			Total 100%

Figure 12-4. Wallace Wallet Works Chart A-2, Sorted by Weight

A-2

Quality Characteristics	Fits in pocket	Fits in purse	Holds cards	Holds cash	Holds checks	Holds letters	Holds pictures	Provides compartments	Provides secret storage	Provides sections	Quality Characteristic Weight
Smoothness		◯ 39	△ 13	◯ 39		△ 13	△ 13	◎ 117	◎ 117	△ 13	13
Texture	◯ 15	◯ 15						△ 5			5
Taper	◯ 12	△ 4									4
Contour	△ 4	△ 4									4
Width			◎ 45					△ 5		△ 5	5
Weight		△ 7		◯ 21							7
Thickness	◯ 54	△ 18			◎ 162			◯ 54			18
Length		◯ 6									2
Compartmentability	△ 23		◯ 69	△ 23	◎ 207			◎ 207	◯ 69	◯ 69	23
Foldability	△ 5							△ 5	◯ 15		5
Depth of compartments			◎ 81			△ 9	△ 9		◯ 27		9
Clearness			◎ 45			◎ 45	◎ 45	◯ 15			5
Column Totals	113	87	259	83	369	67	67	408	213	102	Total 1768
Function Weight %	6	5	15	5	21	3	4	23	13	6	Total 100%

Strong Relationship: ◎ 9
Medium Relationship: ◯ 3
Weak Relationship: △ 1

Figure 12-5. Wallace Wallet Works Chart A-2, Sorted Alphabetically

The software should allow subsets of data to be easily formed so that additional work or analysis can be performed by sub-teams. Large QFD projects are often broken into smaller work groups requiring this function. Subsets should be able to be defined by the team and still maintain their relationship to the original chart. An example of a working subset is shown in figure 12-6.

Functions

A-2

Strong Relationship: ◎ 9

Medium Relationship: ○ 3

Weak Relationship: △ 1

Quality Characteristics — Accessibility

		Holds cash (1)	Holds pictures (2)	Holds checks (3)	Holds cards (4)	Holds letters (5)	Quality Characteristic Weight
Length	1				○ 6		2
Compartmentability	2	△ 23		◎ 207	○ 69		23
Foldability	3						5
Depth of compartments	4		△ 9		◎ 81	△ 9	9
Clearness	5		◎ 45		◎ 45	◎ 45	5

Figure 12-6. Wallace Wallet Works Chart A-2, A Working Subset

Data entry as well as entering the relationships should be easy and graphical. You should have the option of working in either a list mode or a matrix mode for data entry and display. The list mode is easier to understand for most people as all data is presented across the screen. However, some people prefer the visual presentation of the matrix for data and relationship entry. Both modes of entry are shown in figure 12-7.

Functions

A-2

Strong Relationship: ◎ 9
Medium Relationship: ○ 3
Weak Relationship: △ 1

Quality Characteristics	Provides compartments	Provides sections	Provides secret storage	Fits in pocket	Fits in purse	Holds cash	Holds pictures	Holds checks	Holds cards			Quality Characteristic Weight
Smoothness	◎ 117	△ 13	◎ 117		○ 39	○ 39	△ 13		△ 13			
Texture	△ 5			○ 15	○ 15							
Taper				○ 12	△ 4							
Contour				△ 4	△ 4							
Width	△ 5	△ 5							◎ 45			
Weight					△ 7	○ 21						
Thickness	○ 54				○ 54	△ 18		◎ 162				
Length									○ 6			
Compartmentability	◎ 207	○ 69	○ 69	△ 23		△ 23		◎ 207	○ 69			
Foldability	△ 5	○ 15		△ 5								
Depth of compartments				○ 27			△ 9		◎ 81			
Clearness	○ 15							◎ 45	◎ 45			
Column Totals	408	102	213	113	87	83	67	369	259			Total
Function Weight %	23	6	13	6	5	5	4	21	15			Total

Holds letters

Figure 12-7. Wallace Wallet Works Chart A-2, Sorted by Relationship

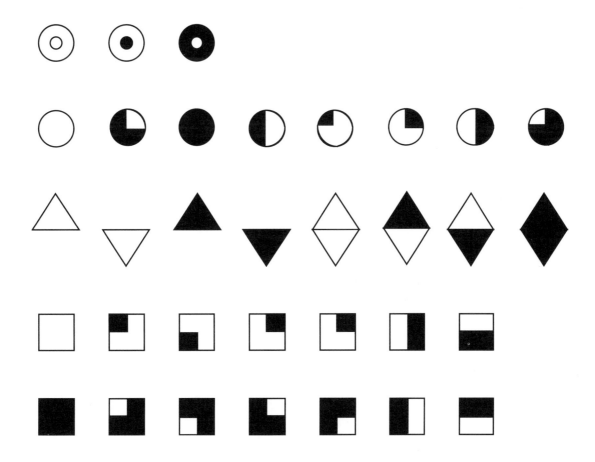

These are the most commonly used symbols. However, all ASCII characters should be able to be entered.

Figure 12-8. QFD Symbols

The team members should have control of the colors and symbols displayed and printed by the software in all matrices. The number and type of symbols used in any matrix should not be limited by the software; the team should be able to design its own custom symbols. Examples of different symbols are shown in figure 12-8.

It should be easy to transfer the information contained in one matrix to other matrices.

Once information is shared between matrices, it should be linked. The software should offer the option of changing the information in all linked matrices if information is changed in any one matrix. These linked matrices should also be identified to allow the team to assess the effect of proposed changes on other matrices prior to actually making the changes. One example of information in linked matrices and how changes can affect matrices is shown in figure 12-9.

A-2

Functions

Strong Relationship: ◎ 9

Medium Relationship: ○ 3

Weak Relationship: △ 1

Quality Characteristics	Provides compartments	Provides sections	Provides secret storage	Fits in pocket	Fits in purse	Holds cash	Displays pictures	Holds checks	Holds cards	Holds letters			Quality Characteristic Weight
Smoothness	◎ 117	△ 13		◎ 117	○ 39	○ 39	△ 13		△ 13	△ 13			13
Texture	△ 5			○ 15	○ 15								5
Taper				○ 12	△ 4								4
Contour				△ 4	△ 4								4
Width	△ 5	△ 5							◎ 45				5
Weight					△ 7	○ 21							7
Thickness	○ 54			○ 54	△ 18			◎ 162					18
Length									○ 6				2
Compartmentability	◎ 207	○ 69	○ 69	△ 23		△ 23		◎ 207	○ 69				23
Foldability	△ 5	○ 15		△ 5									5
Depth of compartments			○ 27					△ 9	◎ 81	△ 9			9
Clearness	○ 15						◎ 45		◎ 45	◎ 45			5
Column Totals	408	102	96	230	87	83	67	369	259	67			Total 1768
Function Weight %	23	6	5	13	5	5	4	21	15	3			Total 100%

Figure 12-9. Wallace Wallet Works Chart A-2

If the function in D-2, for example, is changed from "holds pictures" to "displays pictures," the change will impact all other matrices that include functions such as ASA-2. These changes should be noted by the software prior to making them.

Printing and plotting should be easily accomplished and all required printer drivers should be easily accessed. Print size should be controllable to enable optimum viewing by those requiring hard copy output.

The software should be able to import files from other programs and export its output to other programs to enable the information to be incorporated into reports and to be processed by other programs.

None of the software packages currently available meets all of these criteria. However, any QFD software package will simplify the QFD process and will improve the communication among team members and others who are not on the team. Software also allows subteams to work on portions of the project at their own pace, thereby simplifying the QFD process.

QFD/CAPTURE™, developed by International TechneGroup, Incorporated (ITI), comes the closest to meeting the above criteria at this time. In addition, ITI appears committed to continued research of QFD and integrating that research into updated QFD software products. For this reason, GOAL/QPC recommends and sells QFD/CAPTURE™.

Chapter 13

The Wallace Wallet Watch Works
A Supplementary QFD Case Study

This case study is similar to the Wallace Wallet Works presented in Chapter 7, but uses a watch rather than a wallet as the product for a QFD team to develop. The Wallace Watch Works is a self-contained, interactive exercise that a facilitator or trainer can use to involve participants in the methodology of QFD. The facilitator should mention to the participants that the primary focus of this case study is "hands-on" experience with the process and tools of QFD. This case study has the same associated benefits as the Wallace Wallet Works in Chapter 7. The QFD chart development is similar to that used in the Wallace Wallet Works and therefore is not provided for this case study.

QFD

QUALITY FUNCTION DEPLOYMENT

CASE STUDY:

"THE WALLACE WATCH WORKS"

The Wallace Watch Works: A QFD Case Study

The Wallace Watch Works is a one-product company founded in 1930. Its product is an inexpensive watch with a plastic band. The front of the watch is imprinted with the faces of popular children's characters or actors.

The company's annual sales last year were 18 million dollars. The company has consistently maintained a ten-percent profit margin. All sales are currently made in the United States. The company has 500 employees and is located in Massachusetts in its own 50,000 square foot manufacturing plant.

History

1930	Founded by William Wilhelm Wallace
1930s	Gene Autry Watches
1940s	Roy Rogers Watches
1950s	Elvis Watches
1960s	Beatles Watches
1970s	Flintstone Watches
1980s	Ronald Reagan Watches
1989	Batman Watches
1990	Bart Simpson Watches
1991	Desert Storm Camouflage Watches

Case Problem

The new president of the Wallace Watch Works, Wilamena Wilbur Wallace, is concerned that foreign competition is slowly eroding the company's market share by producing unlicensed copies of its products. The company recently completed a five-year business plan with a goal of expanding from a one-product to a multi-product line. The plan is to expand sales by attracting new customers and by penetrating foreign markets. The company wants to develop a new watch that will appeal to adults in both the United States and foreign markets. The marketing department has developed a product requirement document outlining what this new watch should be like.

Product Requirement: New Adult Watch

- World class.
- Appealing to both men and women.
- Easily visible.
- Legible in the dark.
- Attractive.
- Durable.
- Rugged.
- Accurate.
- Constructed of high-quality material.

Assignment

The Wallace Watch Works has selected your team to provide Quality Function Deployment consulting services to help develop the new product. Attachment 13-1 depicts the current product and its specifications. Your team has agreed as a first phase to develop Chart A-1 detailing the following:

1. Voice of the Customer

- Identify who the potential customers are.
- Brainstorm the voice of the customer.
- Use the customer's language.
- Try for positive, complete statements.
- No one-word statements.
- Arrange using an Affinity Diagram.
- Screen the quality data to be sure it represents the voice of the customer. Remove any functions, quality characteristics, etc., and replace with demanded

quality items. Use the attached QFD Voice of the Customer Table as a guide (Attachments 13-2 and 13-3).
- Analyze the demanded quality items to two levels in a Tree Diagram (four to five header cards with four to five second-level items).

2. Rank the Customer Demanded Quality
- Provide a ranking for each of the second level of detail demanded quality items on a scale of one (low) to three (medium) to five (high) for importance. Use the levels two and four as compromises to reach consensus.

3. Company Now and Competitive Analysis
- Use the watches of each person in your team for this step.
  - The worst-looking watch in the group is the company's product now. This is the way the product is coming off the assembly line today.
  - Establish a rating for the "company now watch" versus each of the second-level demanded quality items with the same scale that was used in the customer importance ratings.
  - The two best-looking watches represent your competition. Develop a rating for each of these versus the demanded quality items using the same scale.

4. Company Plan
- For each second-level demanded quality item, determine where the company should be in the future. Take into account the company's strategic plan, where the competition is, and the level of importance to the customer.

5. Ratio of Improvement
- Divide the company plan rating by the company now rating.

6. Sales Point
- Review the company plan rating versus its corresponding demanded quality items to determine its sales point. A strong sales point (1.5) would be exciting quality that the customer would be delighted with and buy. A medium sales point (1.2) would be something that might intrigue the customer, but not cause compulsive buying.
- All other sales points are given a value of 1.0 and are referred to as ho-hum sales points.

7. Calculate the Absolute Weight
- Multiply the rating of importance by the rate of improvement by the sales point. Then sum the resultants down the column. This process step allows us to factor into the voice of the customer the company's improvement plans plus our indicators of marketing advantage. This composite score is more inclusive of key demanded quality items than just using the voice of the customer alone.

8. Demand Weight
- Divide the absolute weight column total into each individual item in the column and convert to a percentage. Identify the top three to five demanded quality items.

9. Quality Characteristics
- Quality characteristics are measurable items by which we ensure demanded quality is met.

- Arrange them into a three-level Tree Diagram.
- Pick ten items from the third level of the Tree to be used in the matrix.
- Develop through brainstorming a list of quality characteristics.
- Remember that quality characteristics are measurable items.
- Avoid specifying test parameters. Instead, use the test purpose.

10. **Relationships**
   - Develop the relationship matrix between the demanded quality items and the quality characteristics.
   - Use the following relationships:

   ◎ = 9 (strong relationship)

   ○ = 3 (medium relationship)

   △ = 1 (possible relationship)

   - Do not force relationships.
   - Multiply each relationship value by the corresponding demanded weights and record them in that cell.
   - Sum each column and then total each of the sums.
   - Change each column sum to a percentage.
   - Identify the top three to five quality characteristics.

The entire QFD case study must be completed in three hours, including your presentation to the Wallace Watch Works management. The Wallace Watch Works is committed to this concept of new product development. To show its commitment, the company has agreed to have a representative available for consultation throughout the case study for clarification. The representative is John Wallace Moran, Jr. (great-grandson of the founder) or your instructor (a distant cousin). Feel free to call upon the company representative at any time during the case study.

Attachments

Attachment 13-1:
   Product Specifications

Attachment 13-2:
   Voice of the Customer Table, Part 1

Attachment 13-3:
   Voice of the Customer Table, Part 2

Attachment 13-4:
   Chart A-1

Attachment 13-5:
   Generic Quality Table

Attachment 13-6:
   Definitions

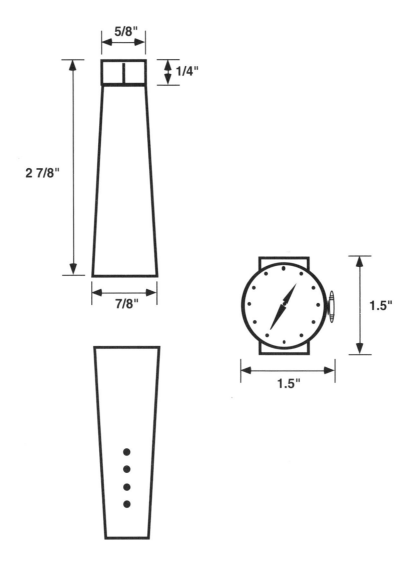

Attachment 13-1 Product Sepcifications

I.D.	Customer Characteristics (who)		Voice of the Customer	Use										
				what		when		where		why		how		
	I/E	Data		I/E	Data	I/E	Data	I/E	Data	I/E	Data	I/E	Data

Attachment 13-2 Voice of the Customer Table, Part 1

Reworded Data	Demanded Quality	Quality Characteristics	Function	Reliability	Comments

Attachment 13-2 Vocie of the Customer Table, Part 2

Quality Characteristics

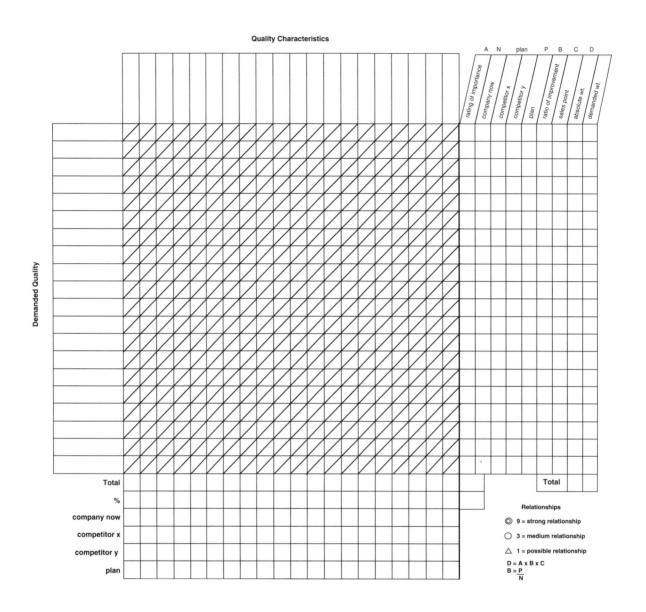

Attachment 13-4 Chart A-1

Quality Characteristics

Relationships

◎ 9 = strong relationship

◯ 3 = medium relationship

△ 1 = possible relationship

Demanded Quality

Total	
%	
company now	
competitor x	
competitor y	
plan	

Attachment 13-5 Generic Quality Table

Attachment 13-6:
QFD Definitions

Demanded Quality

Derived positive statement of what the customer wants and needs.

Quality Characteristics

Measurable items that ensure demanded quality requirements will be met.

Functions

Statements of what the product does. Demanded quality items that contain many key items of which only the producer is aware.

Concepts

When decomposing the product these represent the first level of detail. These are the concepts.

Elements

The next level of detail under the concepts; the second level of detail. An element is an item needed to enable the proposed concepts.

Chapter 14

Summary

This text was developed to assist those facilitating and training in Quality Function Deployment. The text begins with the role of management in the QFD process. Management must nurture, maintain, and continually act in a manner that is supportive of the process. These management actions are vital for the long-term success of any QFD program. Management must lead by example and through involvement. It cannot simply delegate tasks to the facilitator.

Management's role in the QFD process is to:

1. Understand the QFD process.

2. Define the purpose of the QFD project.

3. Prioritize and pre-plan which projects the QFD process will be used on:
   - Who
   - What
   - When
   - Why
   - Where
   - How

4. Develop for the selected QFD projects:
   - Objectives
   - Scope
   - Expectations
   - Goals

5. Appoint a program manager for the project selected for QFD analysis. This program manager is responsible for driving the QFD study and integrating it into the product development process. This responsibility should not be delegated to the facilitator.

The program manager responsible for the team's success needs a facilitator to assist. The facilitator's function is to make certain the QFD effort goes smoothly, to coordinate and set up the meetings, to help the program manager surmount hurdles, to prevent wheel-spinning, and to keep the project on track.

6. Top management and the program manager must pick the members of the QFD study team, including the facilitator.

7. Management must provide the QFD team with a charter for the project. This should be a written statement describing:
   - Goals
   - Objectives
   - Expectations
   - Scope

8. Management must empower the QFD team which includes:
   - Power
   - Permission
   - Protection

9. Management must be committed and involved in the QFD process. This includes asking relevant questions, such as:
   - How did you determine who the customer is?
   - How did you determine de manded quality?
   - How did you do competitive analysis?
   - When did you last survey your customer?
   - What are the major conclusions from the study?

The facilitator's role is one of a coordinator who helps the QFD team complete its objectives in a timely manner. The facilitator has six vital roles to perform in any QFD study as outlined in Chapter 2:
   - Planner
   - Guide
   - Cheerleader
   - Coach
   - Arbitrator
   - Soothsayer

These roles are separate and distinct from those of management but just as vital to the success of the program. Successful implementation of a QFD program requires commitment, support and nurturing by management, and coordination and follow-up by the organization's facilitators.

Glossary

Affinity Diagram:
A tool used to identify relationships within large amounts of data.

Capability Deployment:
A process that identifies factors that must be successfully met in new product or service development. Charts C-1' and C-1" are used for this process.

Cause and Effect Diagram:
A graphing tool used to identify quality characteristics from demanded quality items in the QFD process. The Cause and Effect Diagram is adapted to focus the QFD team on one demanded quality element at a time.

Concept:
A method for achieving functions. Concepts are identified during the concept deployment process.

Concept Deployment:
A process to define alternatives for achieving functions. Chart C-3 is used for this process.

Conceptual Level Design:
A process that uses concept deployment and capability deployment to identify methods for and alternatives to achieving functions needed by the customer in a product or service.

Demanded Quality:
The conversion of the voice of the customer into statements that are understandable by the organization.

Demanded Quality Deployment:
A process that identifies the relationships between demanded quality items and quality characteristics and converts the degree of importance for demanded quality into the degree of importance for quality characteristics. Chart A-1 is used for this process.

Element:
An item needed for achieving the best concepts. Elements are identified during the element deployment process.

Element Deployment:
A process that identifies items needed for achieving concepts and defines the relationships between those items and quality characteristics. Chart A-4 is used for this process.

Element Failure Mode Deployment:
A process that identifies the relationships between elements and their failure modes. Chart D-4 is used for this process.

Element Level Design:
A process that uses element deployment and element failure mode deployment to identify

the items needed for achieving the best concepts.

Facilitator:
A coordinator of the planning, design, execution, and completion of the QFD project.

Failure Mode:
The inability of a product or service to satisfy its intended task.

Fault Tree:
A graphing tool used to identify concepts that cause defects in a product or service.

Functions:
Tasks that are necessary for the product or service to be deliverable and acceptable to the customer.

Function Deployment:
A process that identifies the tasks necessary to meet demanded quality, and identifies the relationships between functions, demanded quality items, and quality characteristics. Function deployment converts the degree of importance for each demanded quality item and quality characteristic to the degree of importance for each function. Charts B-1 and A-2 are used for this process.

Function Tree:
A graphing tool used to identify concepts that are methods of achieving functions needed in a product or service.

Market Planning:
A process that converts the voice of the customer into a marketing plan. The Voice of the Customer Table is used for this process.

Quality Characteristic:
A measurable item that determines if demanded quality items will be met.

Quality Function Deployment (QFD):
A structured and disciplined process that provides a means to identify and carry the voice of the customer through each stage of product development and implementation. This process can be deployed horizontally through marketing, product planning, engineering, manufacturing, service, and all other departments in an organization involved in product development.

Radar Chart:
A graphing technique used in QFD Readiness Assessment. Each spoke on a radar chart represents one of the questions in the QFD Readiness Assessment.

Reliability:
The likelihood that a product or service will satisfy its intended purpose for a specified time period.

Reliability Deployment:
A process that describes failure modes for a product or service based upon demanded quality or function, and identifies the associated relationships to help identify failure modes to be carried forward into further analysis. Charts D-1 and D-2 are used for this process.

Reworded Data:
A process of extracting all possible demands that a customer may include in a statement of wants and needs. The multiple demands

contained in the customer words are singularized via the rewording activity. This
process also includes the analysis of usage.

System Level Design:
A process that uses demanded quality deployment, function deployment, reliability
deployment, and part of capability deployment to determine the concept of a product
or service.

Tree Diagram:
A graphing tool that maps out in increasing
detail the full range of paths and tasks that
need to be accomplished in order to achieve a
primary goal and every related subgoal.

Voice of the Customer:
Communication of the customer's wants and
needs that may include demanded quality,
functions, reliability, and other information
relative to the products or services the customer requires.

Voice of the Customer Table (VOCT):
The organization of customer characteristics
into categories to analyze how a customer
plans to use a product or service.

Index

A

Absolute weight
  Chart A-1, part 1   79
  Wallace Wallet Works   52
Affinity Diagram
  defined   145
  for customer demand   82
  use in QFD   45
  Wallace Wallet Works   52

B

Baselining
  QFD process   7
  results   15
  visual images developed   15
Brainstorming
  customer demand   83
  voice of the customer   45
  Wallace Wallet Works   97
Breakthrough
  breakthrough phase   35

C

Capability
  deployment   70
Capability deployment
  defined   145
Cause and Effect Diagram
  construction   60
  defined   145
  for customer demand   82
  voice of the customer   59, 60
  Wallace Wallet Works   82
Chart A-1   77
  part 1   77
    Wallace Wallet Works   77, 81
  part 2   83
    Wallace Wallet Works   86
Chart A-2   91
  Wallace Wallet Works   92

Chart A-3'   101
  Wallace Wallet Works   102
Chart A-4   103
  Wallace Wallet Works   105
Chart B-1   89
  Wallace Wallet Works   90
Chart C-3   96
  Wallace Wallet Works   98
Chart D-2   93
  Wallace Wallet Works   95
Chart D-4   106
  Wallace Wallet Works   108
Chart E-3   99
  Wallace Wallet Works   100
Column total
  Chart C-3   96
  Chart D-2   94
Column totals
  Chart B-1   89
Column weight
  Chart A-2   91
Comments
  VOCT, part 2   62
Company now
  Chart A-1, part 1   79
  Chart A-1, part 2   83
Company plan
  Wallace Wallet Works   52
Competitive analysis
  Wallace Wallet Works   52
Concept
  defined   145, 57
  deployment   71
Concept deployment
  defined   145
Concept weight
  Chart C-3   96
Concepts
  Chart C-3   96
Conceptual level design
  defined   145

Cross-Functional Management   1
Customer demand
    Affinity Diagram   82
    brainstorming   83
    Cause and Effect Diagram   82
    Tree Diagram   83
    Wallace Wallet Works   75

D

Data
    VOCT, part 1   62
Demand weight
    Wallace Wallet Works   52
Demanded quality
    Chart B-1   89
    defined   145, 57
    deployment   69
    VOCT, part 2   62
    Wallace Wallet Works   52
Demanded quality deployment
    defined   145
Demanded quality table
    Chart A-1, part 1
        Wallace Wallet Works   77
Demanded quality tree
    Wallace Wallet Works   80
Demanded quality weight
    Chart B-1   89
Demanded weight
    Chart A-1, part 1   81
Design systems
    comparison of old and new   29

E

Element
    Chart A-4   103
    Chart D-4   106
    defined   145, 57
    deployment   71
    Wallace Wallet Works   104
Element deployment
    defined   145
Element failure mode
    Chart D-4   106
    deployment   71
Element failure mode deployment
    defined   145
Element failure mode weight

Chart D-4   106
Element fault tree
    Wallace Wallet Works   107
Element level design
    defined   145
    flow   71
Element weight
    Chart A-4   103
    Chart D-4   106

F

Facilitator
    defined   146
    function of   3
    introducing QFD   7
    meeting checklist   4
    meeting planning   3
    role in QFD   1
    teaching history of QFD   17
Failure mode
    defined   146
Failure mode weight
    Chart D-2   94
Fault tree
    defined   146
Function
    Chart A-2   91
    Chart B-1   89
    Chart D-2   94
    defined   146, 57
    deployment   70
    VOCT, part 2   62
Function deployment
    defined   146
Function tree
    building   88
    defined   146, 88
    Wallace Wallet Works   88
Function weight
    Chart A-2   91
    Chart B-1   89
    Chart D-2   94
    comparing Charts A-2 and B-1   93

G

Generic quality table
    Wallace Wallet Works   56

I

I.D.
  VOCT part 1 62

J

Japanese QFD
  results of 27

K

Key concepts
  Chart E-3 99

M

Market planning
  defined 146
  flow 69
Matrices
  Matrix of Matrices 68

N

New functions
  Chart B-1 89

O

Overhead presentation 21

P

Plan
  Chart A-1, part 1 79
Plan (target value)
  Chart A-1, part 2 83
Pockets of excellence
  defined 12
Product design
  comparison of old and new 29
Product failure mode
  Chart D-2 94
Product fault tree
  Wallace Wallet Works 94
Program manager
  involvement in QFD 43

Q

QFD. *See* Quality Function Deployment

QFD team
  selection of 44
QIT
  reference materials 15
  used in introducing QFD 15
Quality
  defined 23
Quality characteristics
  Chart A-2 91
  Chart A-4 103
  Chart C-3 96
  Chart E-3 99
  defined 146
  VOCT part 2 62
  Wallace Wallet Works 52, 57
  weight
    Chart A-2 91
    Chart A-4 103
  weight computation 83
Quality characteristics table
  Chart A-1, part 2 83
Quality characteristics weight
  Chart C-3 96
Quality Function Deployment
  baselining process 7
  benefits 46
  breakthrough phase 35
  case study
    Wallace Wallet Works 49
  defined 146, 25, 1
  describing the product/service 33
  history 17
  implementation 37
  software
    QFD/CAPTURE™ 131
    requirements 121
  voice of the customer
    Affinity Diagram 45
    obtaining 44
Quality improvement process
  reference materials 15
Quality improvement team. *See* QIT

R

Radar chart
  defined 146
  QFD readiness assessment 11

Rate of improvement
    Chart A-1, part 1   79
Rating of importance
    Chart A-1, part 1   79
Ratio of improvement
    Wallace Wallet Works   52
Readiness assessment   7
    pockets of excellence   12
    radar chart   11
Relationship matrix
    Chart A-1, part 2   83
Relationships
    Chart A-2   91
    Chart A-4   103
    Chart B-1   89
    Chart C-3   96
    Chart D-2   94
    Chart D-4   106
    Chart E-3   99
    Wallace Wallet Works   53
Reliability
    defined   146
    deployment   70
    VOCT, part 2   62
Reliability deployment
    defined   146

S

Sales point
    Chart A-1, part 1   79
    Wallace Wallet Works   52
Subsystem level design   70
System level design   69
    defined   147

T

Target value
    Chart E-3   99
Tree Diagram
    customer demand   83
    defined   147
    Wallace Wallet Works   84, 53

U

United States QFD
    results   39

V

Visual image
    developed through baselining   15
VOCT. *See* Voice of the customer
Voice of the customer
    Affinity Diagram   45
    analysis   69
    brainstorming   45
    Cause and Effect Diagram   60
    defined   147
    obtaining   59, 44
    organizing   45
    table   61
    table, part 1   62
        Wallace Wallet Works   75
    table, part 2   62
    Wallace Wallet Works   51
Voice of the Customer Table
    defined   147
    purpose   63
    Wallace Wallet Works   54

W

Wallace Wallet Works   51